50 Global Taco Fusion Recipes for Home

By: Kelly Johnson

Table of Contents

- Miso-Glazed Salmon Tacos with Pickled Daikon
- Mediterranean Gyro Tacos with Tzatziki Drizzle
- Korean BBQ Beef Bulgogi Tacos with Kimchi Slaw
- Thai Red Curry Shrimp Tacos with Mango Salsa
- Mexican Street Corn Elote Tacos with Cotija Cheese
- Indian Butter Chicken Tacos with Cilantro Chutney
- Brazilian Feijoada Tacos with Orange Avocado Salsa
- Moroccan Spiced Lamb Tacos with Harissa Yogurt
- Hawaiian Poke Tuna Tacos with Pineapple Salsa
- Peruvian Lomo Saltado Tacos with Aji Amarillo Sauce
- Japanese Teriyaki Chicken Tacos with Wasabi Mayo
- French Ratatouille Tacos with Herbed Goat Cheese
- Caribbean Jerk Pork Tacos with Pineapple Salsa
- Turkish Lamb Kofta Tacos with Cucumber Yogurt Sauce
- Vietnamese Banh Mi Tacos with Pickled Daikon and Carrots
- Greek Souvlaki Tacos with Tzatziki and Feta
- Argentinian Chimichurri Steak Tacos with Grilled Corn Salsa
- Thai Green Curry Vegetable Tacos with Peanut Sauce
- Spanish Paella Tacos with Saffron Aioli
- African Peri-Peri Chicken Tacos with Mango Avocado Relish
- Irish Corned Beef and Cabbage Tacos with Mustard Sauce
- Indonesian Satay Chicken Tacos with Peanut Drizzle
- Lebanese Shawarma Tacos with Garlic Tahini Sauce
- Mexican Mole Chicken Tacos with Sesame Seeds
- Italian Caprese Tacos with Balsamic Glaze
- Cuban Ropa Vieja Tacos with Plantain Chips
- Filipino Adobo Pork Tacos with Pineapple Salsa
- Swedish Swedish Meatball Tacos with Lingonberry Sauce
- Bangladeshi Fish Curry Tacos with Cilantro Yogurt
- Australian Grilled Kangaroo Tacos with Bush Tomato Salsa
- Russian Beef Stroganoff Tacos with Sour Cream and Dill
- Israeli Falafel Tacos with Hummus and Pickled Radishes
- Canadian Poutine Tacos with Gravy and Cheese Curds
- Jamaican Jerk Jackfruit Tacos with Mango Salsa
- Chinese Peking Duck Tacos with Hoisin Plum Sauce

- Portuguese Bacalhau Tacos with Olive Tapenade
- Scottish Haggis Tacos with Neeps and Tatties Mash
- Peruvian Ceviche Tacos with Aji Amarillo Crema
- German Sauerbraten Tacos with Red Cabbage Slaw
- Nigerian Jollof Rice Tacos with Spicy Tomato Relish
- Swiss Fondue Tacos with Gruyère and Caramelized Onions
- Thai Massaman Curry Beef Tacos with Peanut Crunch
- Turkish Lahmacun-Inspired Lamb Tacos with Sumac Yogurt
- Polish Pierogi Tacos with Potato and Cheddar Filling
- Brazilian Moqueca Tacos with Coconut-Lime Drizzle
- Hawaiian Loco Moco Tacos with Sunny-Side-Up Egg
- Moroccan Lamb Tagine Tacos with Apricot Chutney
- Filipino Halo-Halo Tacos with Ube Ice Cream
- Canadian Butter Tart Tacos with Pecans and Maple Syrup
- Malaysian Nasi Lemak Tacos with Sambal Belacan

Miso-Glazed Salmon Tacos with Pickled Daikon

Ingredients:

For the Miso-Glazed Salmon:

- 1 pound salmon fillets, skinless, cut into taco-sized portions
- 3 tablespoons white miso paste
- 2 tablespoons mirin (sweet rice wine)
- 2 tablespoons soy sauce
- 1 tablespoon rice vinegar
- 1 tablespoon maple syrup or honey
- 1 tablespoon sesame oil
- 2 cloves garlic, minced
- 1 teaspoon grated ginger

For Pickled Daikon:

- 1 cup daikon radish, julienned
- 1/2 cup rice vinegar
- 1 tablespoon sugar
- 1 teaspoon salt

For Tacos:

- Small corn or flour tortillas
- Fresh cilantro leaves, chopped
- Sliced green onions
- Toasted sesame seeds
- Lime wedges for serving

Instructions:

1. Marinate the Salmon:

    In a bowl, whisk together miso paste, mirin, soy sauce, rice vinegar, maple syrup or honey, sesame oil, minced garlic, and grated ginger.
    Place salmon fillets in a shallow dish and pour the miso glaze over them. Allow to marinate for at least 30 minutes in the refrigerator.

2. Prepare Pickled Daikon:

In a small bowl, combine rice vinegar, sugar, and salt. Stir until sugar and salt are dissolved.

Add julienned daikon to the vinegar mixture, ensuring the daikon is fully submerged. Allow it to pickle for at least 15-20 minutes.

3. Cook the Salmon:

Preheat your oven to 400°F (200°C).

Place marinated salmon fillets on a baking sheet lined with parchment paper.

Bake for about 12-15 minutes or until the salmon is cooked through and flakes easily.

4. Assemble Tacos:

Warm tortillas according to package instructions.

Place a piece of miso-glazed salmon in each tortilla.

Top with pickled daikon, chopped cilantro, sliced green onions, and toasted sesame seeds.

Serve with lime wedges on the side.

Enjoy the delicious fusion of flavors in these Miso-Glazed Salmon Tacos with Pickled Daikon!

Mediterranean Gyro Tacos with Tzatziki Drizzle

Ingredients:

For the Gyro Seasoning:

- 1 pound lamb or beef, thinly sliced
- 2 teaspoons dried oregano
- 1 teaspoon dried thyme
- 1 teaspoon ground cumin
- 1 teaspoon ground coriander
- 1 teaspoon garlic powder
- Salt and black pepper to taste
- 2 tablespoons olive oil

For Tzatziki Drizzle:

- 1 cup Greek yogurt
- 1 cucumber, finely diced
- 2 cloves garlic, minced
- 1 tablespoon fresh dill, chopped
- 1 tablespoon lemon juice
- Salt and black pepper to taste

For Tacos:

- Small corn or flour tortillas
- Cherry tomatoes, halved
- Red onion, thinly sliced
- Fresh parsley, chopped
- Feta cheese, crumbled
- Kalamata olives, sliced (optional)

Instructions:

1. Prepare Gyro Seasoning:

   In a bowl, combine dried oregano, dried thyme, ground cumin, ground coriander, garlic powder, salt, and black pepper.
   Toss the thinly sliced lamb or beef in the seasoning mix until evenly coated.

2. Cook Gyro Meat:

Heat olive oil in a skillet over medium-high heat.
Cook the seasoned lamb or beef slices until browned and cooked to your liking, about 3-5 minutes per side.

3. Prepare Tzatziki Drizzle:

In a bowl, combine Greek yogurt, finely diced cucumber, minced garlic, chopped fresh dill, lemon juice, salt, and black pepper.
Mix well and refrigerate until ready to use.

4. Assemble Tacos:

Warm tortillas according to package instructions.
Place gyro meat on each tortilla.
Top with cherry tomatoes, red onion slices, chopped fresh parsley, crumbled feta cheese, and sliced Kalamata olives if desired.
Drizzle with tzatziki sauce.

5. Serve:

Enjoy your Mediterranean Gyro Tacos with Tzatziki Drizzle immediately. Serve with extra tzatziki on the side for dipping, if desired.

These tacos bring the classic flavors of a Greek gyro into a fun and portable form. Bon appétit!

Korean BBQ Beef Bulgogi Tacos with Kimchi Slaw

Ingredients:

For the Korean BBQ Beef Bulgogi:

- 1 pound thinly sliced beef (ribeye or sirloin)
- 1/2 cup soy sauce
- 3 tablespoons brown sugar
- 2 tablespoons mirin (sweet rice wine)
- 2 tablespoons sesame oil
- 2 cloves garlic, minced
- 1 tablespoon ginger, grated
- 2 green onions, sliced
- 1 tablespoon toasted sesame seeds
- 1 tablespoon vegetable oil (for cooking)

For the Kimchi Slaw:

- 2 cups cabbage, thinly shredded
- 1 cup kimchi, chopped
- 2 tablespoons rice vinegar
- 1 tablespoon sesame oil
- 1 tablespoon honey or sugar
- Salt to taste

For Tacos:

- Small corn or flour tortillas
- Sliced cucumber
- Fresh cilantro leaves
- Lime wedges for serving

Instructions:

1. Prepare Korean BBQ Beef Bulgogi:

   In a bowl, whisk together soy sauce, brown sugar, mirin, sesame oil, minced garlic, grated ginger, sliced green onions, and toasted sesame seeds.
   Add the thinly sliced beef to the marinade and allow it to marinate for at least 30 minutes.

2. Cook Korean BBQ Beef Bulgogi:

Heat vegetable oil in a skillet or wok over medium-high heat.
Cook the marinated beef slices until browned and cooked through, about 2-3 minutes per side.

3. Prepare Kimchi Slaw:

In a bowl, combine thinly shredded cabbage and chopped kimchi.
In a small bowl, whisk together rice vinegar, sesame oil, honey or sugar, and salt.
Pour the dressing over the cabbage and kimchi mixture, tossing to coat.

4. Assemble Tacos:

Warm tortillas according to package instructions.
Place Korean BBQ Beef Bulgogi on each tortilla.
Top with kimchi slaw, sliced cucumber, and fresh cilantro leaves.
Serve with lime wedges on the side.

5. Serve:

Enjoy your Korean BBQ Beef Bulgogi Tacos with Kimchi Slaw immediately. The combination of the savory bulgogi and the tangy crunch of kimchi slaw creates a delightful and flavorful taco experience.

Thai Red Curry Shrimp Tacos with Mango Salsa

Ingredients:

For the Thai Red Curry Shrimp:

- 1 pound large shrimp, peeled and deveined
- 2 tablespoons red curry paste
- 1 can (14 oz) coconut milk
- 1 tablespoon fish sauce
- 1 tablespoon soy sauce
- 1 tablespoon brown sugar
- 1 lime, juiced
- 2 tablespoons vegetable oil
- Fresh cilantro, chopped (for garnish)

For the Mango Salsa:

- 1 ripe mango, peeled, pitted, and diced
- 1/2 red onion, finely chopped
- 1 red bell pepper, diced
- 1/4 cup fresh cilantro, chopped
- 1 lime, juiced
- Salt and pepper to taste

For Tacos:

- Small corn or flour tortillas
- Shredded lettuce or cabbage
- Sliced avocado
- Lime wedges for serving

Instructions:

1. Prepare Thai Red Curry Shrimp:

   In a bowl, whisk together red curry paste, coconut milk, fish sauce, soy sauce, brown sugar, and lime juice.
   Heat vegetable oil in a skillet over medium heat.
   Add the shrimp to the skillet and cook for 1-2 minutes on each side until they begin to turn pink.

Pour the red curry mixture over the shrimp and simmer until the shrimp are fully cooked and the sauce thickens.

2. Prepare Mango Salsa:

In a bowl, combine diced mango, chopped red onion, diced red bell pepper, chopped cilantro, lime juice, salt, and pepper.
Mix well and set aside.

3. Assemble Tacos:

Warm tortillas according to package instructions.
Place a spoonful of Thai Red Curry Shrimp on each tortilla.
Top with shredded lettuce or cabbage, a spoonful of mango salsa, and sliced avocado.
Garnish with chopped cilantro and serve with lime wedges on the side.

4. Serve:

Enjoy your Thai Red Curry Shrimp Tacos with Mango Salsa immediately. The combination of the spicy Thai red curry shrimp and the sweet-tangy mango salsa creates a delightful explosion of flavors in every bite.

Mexican Street Corn Elote Tacos with Cotija Cheese

Ingredients:

For the Mexican Street Corn Elote:

- 4 cups corn kernels (fresh or frozen)
- 1/2 cup mayonnaise
- 1/2 cup sour cream
- 1/2 cup cotija cheese, crumbled
- 2 tablespoons lime juice
- 1 teaspoon chili powder
- 1/4 cup fresh cilantro, chopped
- Salt and pepper to taste

For Tacos:

- Small corn or flour tortillas
- Lime wedges for serving
- Extra cotija cheese for garnish
- Fresh cilantro, chopped (for garnish)

Instructions:

1. Prepare Mexican Street Corn Elote:

    In a large skillet over medium heat, cook the corn kernels until they are charred and golden brown, about 5-7 minutes.
    In a bowl, combine mayonnaise, sour cream, crumbled cotija cheese, lime juice, chili powder, chopped cilantro, salt, and pepper.
    Add the cooked corn to the mixture and toss until well coated.

2. Assemble Tacos:

    Warm tortillas according to package instructions.
    Spoon the Mexican Street Corn Elote mixture onto each tortilla.
    Garnish with extra crumbled cotija cheese and chopped cilantro.
    Serve with lime wedges on the side.

3. Serve:

Enjoy your Mexican Street Corn Elote Tacos with Cotija Cheese immediately. These tacos capture the essence of the beloved Mexican street corn with the added convenience of a taco format. The creamy, tangy, and savory flavors make for a delicious and satisfying dish.

Indian Butter Chicken Tacos with Cilantro Chutney

Ingredients:

For the Butter Chicken:

- 1.5 pounds boneless, skinless chicken thighs or breasts, cut into bite-sized pieces
- 1 cup plain yogurt
- 2 tablespoons ginger-garlic paste
- 1 teaspoon ground turmeric
- 1 teaspoon ground cumin
- 1 teaspoon ground coriander
- 1 teaspoon garam masala
- 1 teaspoon chili powder (adjust to taste)
- Salt and pepper to taste
- 2 tablespoons vegetable oil
- 1 large onion, finely chopped
- 3 tomatoes, pureed
- 1/2 cup heavy cream
- 2 tablespoons unsalted butter
- Fresh cilantro, chopped (for garnish)

For the Cilantro Chutney:

- 1 cup fresh cilantro leaves
- 1/2 cup fresh mint leaves
- 1 green chili, chopped (adjust to taste)
- 1 tablespoon ginger, grated
- 1 tablespoon lime juice
- Salt to taste
- Water (as needed)

For Tacos:

- Small corn or flour tortillas
- Sliced red onions
- Sliced tomatoes
- Lime wedges for serving

Instructions:

1. Prepare Butter Chicken:

In a bowl, mix yogurt, ginger-garlic paste, ground turmeric, ground cumin, ground coriander, garam masala, chili powder, salt, and pepper.

Add chicken pieces to the marinade, ensuring they are well-coated. Allow it to marinate for at least 30 minutes.

In a large skillet, heat vegetable oil over medium heat. Add chopped onions and sauté until golden brown.

Add the marinated chicken and cook until browned on all sides.

Stir in tomato puree and cook until the oil starts to separate.

Pour in heavy cream and butter. Simmer for 10-15 minutes until the chicken is cooked through and the sauce thickens.

2. Prepare Cilantro Chutney:

In a blender, combine cilantro leaves, mint leaves, chopped green chili, grated ginger, lime juice, salt, and a splash of water.

Blend until you achieve a smooth chutney consistency. Adjust salt and lime juice to taste.

3. Assemble Tacos:

Warm tortillas according to package instructions.

Spoon Butter Chicken onto each tortilla.

Top with sliced red onions, sliced tomatoes, and chopped cilantro.

Drizzle with Cilantro Chutney.

Serve with lime wedges on the side.

4. Serve:

Enjoy your Indian Butter Chicken Tacos with Cilantro Chutney immediately. The combination of creamy butter chicken and zesty cilantro chutney creates a unique and delicious fusion of Indian and Mexican flavors.

Brazilian Feijoada Tacos with Orange Avocado Salsa

Ingredients:

For the Feijoada:

- 1 pound black beans, soaked overnight and cooked
- 1 pound smoked sausage, sliced
- 1 pound pork shoulder or ribs, cut into chunks
- 1 onion, finely chopped
- 4 cloves garlic, minced
- 2 bay leaves
- 1 teaspoon cumin
- 1 teaspoon paprika
- Salt and black pepper to taste
- 4 cups water or beef broth
- Chopped fresh cilantro (for garnish)

For the Orange Avocado Salsa:

- 2 oranges, peeled and diced
- 2 avocados, diced
- 1 red onion, finely chopped
- 1 jalapeño, seeds removed and finely chopped
- Fresh cilantro, chopped
- Lime juice to taste
- Salt and black pepper to taste

For Tacos:

- Small corn or flour tortillas
- Shredded cabbage or lettuce
- Lime wedges for serving

Instructions:

1. Prepare Feijoada:

   In a large pot, combine black beans, smoked sausage, pork shoulder or ribs, chopped onion, minced garlic, bay leaves, cumin, paprika, salt, and black pepper.
   Pour in water or beef broth to cover the ingredients.

Bring the mixture to a boil, then reduce the heat to low and simmer for 2-3 hours until the beans are tender and the meat is cooked through.
Adjust seasoning as needed. Remove bay leaves before serving.
Garnish with chopped fresh cilantro.

2. Prepare Orange Avocado Salsa:

In a bowl, combine diced oranges, diced avocados, finely chopped red onion, chopped jalapeño, chopped cilantro, lime juice, salt, and black pepper.
Gently toss the ingredients until well combined. Adjust salt and lime juice to taste.

3. Assemble Tacos:

Warm tortillas according to package instructions.
Spoon Feijoada onto each tortilla.
Top with shredded cabbage or lettuce.
Spoon Orange Avocado Salsa over the feijoada.
Serve with lime wedges on the side.

4. Serve:

Enjoy your Brazilian Feijoada Tacos with Orange Avocado Salsa immediately. The combination of the hearty feijoada and the zesty orange avocado salsa creates a unique and delightful fusion of Brazilian and Mexican flavors.

Moroccan Spiced Lamb Tacos with Harissa Yogurt

Ingredients:

For the Moroccan Spiced Lamb:

- 1.5 pounds ground lamb
- 1 onion, finely chopped
- 3 cloves garlic, minced
- 2 teaspoons ground cumin
- 2 teaspoons ground coriander
- 1 teaspoon ground cinnamon
- 1 teaspoon paprika
- 1/2 teaspoon ground ginger
- 1/2 teaspoon cayenne pepper (adjust to taste)
- Salt and black pepper to taste
- 2 tablespoons olive oil
- Fresh cilantro, chopped (for garnish)

For the Harissa Yogurt:

- 1 cup Greek yogurt
- 2 tablespoons harissa paste
- 1 tablespoon lemon juice
- Salt to taste

For Tacos:

- Small corn or flour tortillas
- Sliced cucumber
- Sliced radishes
- Fresh mint leaves
- Lemon wedges for serving

Instructions:

1. Prepare Moroccan Spiced Lamb:

    In a large skillet, heat olive oil over medium heat.
    Add chopped onions and sauté until translucent.
    Add minced garlic and ground lamb. Cook until lamb is browned.

Stir in ground cumin, ground coriander, ground cinnamon, paprika, ground ginger, cayenne pepper, salt, and black pepper. Cook for an additional 2-3 minutes until the spices are fragrant.

Remove from heat and set aside.

2. Prepare Harissa Yogurt:

In a bowl, whisk together Greek yogurt, harissa paste, lemon juice, and salt. Adjust the level of harissa and salt according to your taste.

3. Assemble Tacos:

Warm tortillas according to package instructions.
Spoon the Moroccan Spiced Lamb onto each tortilla.
Top with sliced cucumber, sliced radishes, and fresh mint leaves.
Drizzle with Harissa Yogurt.
Serve with lemon wedges on the side.

4. Serve:

Enjoy your Moroccan Spiced Lamb Tacos with Harissa Yogurt immediately. The combination of the aromatic Moroccan spices, the cooling harissa yogurt, and the freshness of the toppings creates a harmonious and flavorful taco experience.

Hawaiian Poke Tuna Tacos with Pineapple Salsa

Ingredients:

For the Poke Tuna:

- 1 pound sushi-grade tuna, diced
- 1/4 cup soy sauce
- 1 tablespoon sesame oil
- 1 tablespoon rice vinegar
- 1 teaspoon Sriracha (adjust to taste)
- 1 teaspoon honey or agave nectar
- 1 green onion, thinly sliced
- 1 teaspoon sesame seeds
- Fresh cilantro, chopped (for garnish)

For the Pineapple Salsa:

- 1 cup fresh pineapple, diced
- 1/2 red onion, finely chopped
- 1 jalapeño, seeds removed and finely chopped
- 1/4 cup fresh cilantro, chopped
- Juice of 1 lime
- Salt and black pepper to taste

For Tacos:

- Small corn or flour tortillas
- Shredded lettuce or cabbage
- Avocado slices
- Lime wedges for serving

Instructions:

1. Prepare Poke Tuna:

   In a bowl, whisk together soy sauce, sesame oil, rice vinegar, Sriracha, and honey or agave nectar.
   Add diced tuna, sliced green onion, and sesame seeds to the sauce. Toss gently to coat.
   Refrigerate the poke tuna for at least 15-20 minutes to marinate.

2. Prepare Pineapple Salsa:

In a bowl, combine diced pineapple, finely chopped red onion, chopped jalapeño, chopped cilantro, lime juice, salt, and black pepper.
Mix well and set aside.

3. Assemble Tacos:

Warm tortillas according to package instructions.
Spoon shredded lettuce or cabbage onto each tortilla.
Top with marinated Poke Tuna.
Add a generous scoop of Pineapple Salsa.
Garnish with avocado slices and chopped cilantro.
Serve with lime wedges on the side.

4. Serve:

Enjoy your Hawaiian Poke Tuna Tacos with Pineapple Salsa immediately. The combination of the fresh, flavorful poke tuna and the tropical sweetness of pineapple salsa creates a delicious and satisfying taco experience.

Peruvian Lomo Saltado Tacos with Aji Amarillo Sauce

Ingredients:

For the Lomo Saltado:

- 1 pound beef sirloin or tenderloin, thinly sliced
- 2 tablespoons soy sauce
- 2 tablespoons red wine vinegar
- 1 tablespoon vegetable oil
- 1 red onion, thinly sliced
- 1 bell pepper (any color), thinly sliced
- 2 tomatoes, sliced into wedges
- 3 cloves garlic, minced
- 1 teaspoon ground cumin
- 1 teaspoon paprika
- Salt and black pepper to taste
- Fresh cilantro, chopped (for garnish)

For the Aji Amarillo Sauce:

- 2 tablespoons Aji Amarillo paste (Peruvian yellow chili paste)
- 1/2 cup mayonnaise
- 1 tablespoon lime juice
- Salt and black pepper to taste

For Tacos:

- Small corn or flour tortillas
- Cooked white rice
- Fresh cilantro, chopped (for garnish)
- Lime wedges for serving

Instructions:

1. Prepare Lomo Saltado:

    In a bowl, mix sliced beef with soy sauce and red wine vinegar. Set aside to marinate for at least 15-20 minutes.
    Heat vegetable oil in a large skillet over high heat.
    Add marinated beef to the skillet and stir-fry until browned. Remove from the skillet and set aside.

In the same skillet, add a bit more oil if needed. Sauté sliced red onion, bell pepper, and tomato wedges until slightly tender.

Add minced garlic, ground cumin, paprika, salt, and black pepper. Stir-fry for an additional 2 minutes.

Return the cooked beef to the skillet and toss everything together. Cook for another 2-3 minutes until well combined.

Garnish with chopped fresh cilantro.

2. Prepare Aji Amarillo Sauce:

In a bowl, whisk together Aji Amarillo paste, mayonnaise, lime juice, salt, and black pepper.

Adjust the level of Aji Amarillo and salt according to your taste.

3. Assemble Tacos:

Warm tortillas according to package instructions.

Spoon cooked white rice onto each tortilla.

Top with the Lomo Saltado mixture.

Drizzle Aji Amarillo Sauce over the filling.

Garnish with chopped fresh cilantro.

Serve with lime wedges on the side.

4. Serve:

Enjoy your Peruvian Lomo Saltado Tacos with Aji Amarillo Sauce immediately. The combination of the savory Lomo Saltado and the zesty Aji Amarillo Sauce creates a unique and delicious taco experience.

Japanese Teriyaki Chicken Tacos with Wasabi Mayo

Ingredients:

For the Teriyaki Chicken:

- 1 pound boneless, skinless chicken thighs, thinly sliced
- 1/2 cup soy sauce
- 1/4 cup mirin (sweet rice wine)
- 2 tablespoons sake or dry white wine
- 2 tablespoons sugar
- 1 tablespoon vegetable oil
- 2 cloves garlic, minced
- 1 teaspoon grated ginger
- 1 tablespoon cornstarch mixed with 2 tablespoons water (for thickening)

For the Wasabi Mayo:

- 1/2 cup mayonnaise
- 1-2 teaspoons wasabi paste (adjust to taste)
- 1 teaspoon soy sauce
- 1 teaspoon rice vinegar
- 1 teaspoon sugar

For Tacos:

- Small corn or flour tortillas
- Shredded cabbage or lettuce
- Sliced cucumber
- Sesame seeds for garnish
- Green onions, sliced (for garnish)

Instructions:

1. Prepare Teriyaki Chicken:

   In a bowl, whisk together soy sauce, mirin, sake or white wine, sugar, minced garlic, and grated ginger.
   Heat vegetable oil in a skillet over medium-high heat.
   Add thinly sliced chicken to the skillet and cook until browned.
   Pour the teriyaki sauce over the chicken and simmer until the sauce thickens.
   Stir in the cornstarch-water mixture to further thicken the sauce.

Remove from heat and set aside.

2. Prepare Wasabi Mayo:

    In a bowl, combine mayonnaise, wasabi paste, soy sauce, rice vinegar, and sugar.
    Adjust the level of wasabi and sugar according to your taste.

3. Assemble Tacos:

    Warm tortillas according to package instructions.
    Spoon shredded cabbage or lettuce onto each tortilla.
    Top with teriyaki chicken.
    Add sliced cucumber.
    Drizzle with wasabi mayo.
    Garnish with sesame seeds and sliced green onions.

4. Serve:

Enjoy your Japanese Teriyaki Chicken Tacos with Wasabi Mayo immediately. The combination of the sweet and savory teriyaki chicken with the zesty kick of wasabi mayo creates a delicious and flavorful taco experience.

French Ratatouille Tacos with Herbed Goat Cheese

Ingredients:

For the Ratatouille:

- 1 eggplant, diced
- 1 zucchini, diced
- 1 yellow bell pepper, diced
- 1 red bell pepper, diced
- 1 onion, finely chopped
- 3 cloves garlic, minced
- 3 tomatoes, diced
- 2 tablespoons tomato paste
- 2 teaspoons dried thyme
- 1 teaspoon dried rosemary
- Salt and black pepper to taste
- Olive oil for cooking

For the Herbed Goat Cheese:

- 4 ounces goat cheese, softened
- 1 tablespoon fresh parsley, finely chopped
- 1 tablespoon fresh chives, finely chopped
- Salt and black pepper to taste

For Tacos:

- Small corn or flour tortillas
- Fresh arugula or spinach
- Balsamic glaze for drizzling

Instructions:

1. Prepare Ratatouille:

    In a large skillet, heat olive oil over medium heat.
    Add chopped onion and minced garlic, sauté until softened.
    Add diced eggplant, zucchini, bell peppers, and tomatoes to the skillet.
    Stir in tomato paste, dried thyme, dried rosemary, salt, and black pepper.
    Cook until the vegetables are tender but not mushy, about 15-20 minutes.

2. Prepare Herbed Goat Cheese:

> In a bowl, mix softened goat cheese with finely chopped parsley and chives.
> Season with salt and black pepper. Set aside.

3. Assemble Tacos:

> Warm tortillas according to package instructions.
> Spread a generous layer of herbed goat cheese onto each tortilla.
> Spoon ratatouille over the goat cheese layer.
> Top with fresh arugula or spinach.
> Drizzle with balsamic glaze for extra flavor.

4. Serve:

Enjoy your French Ratatouille Tacos with Herbed Goat Cheese immediately. The combination of the rustic ratatouille and the creamy herbed goat cheese creates a sophisticated and delicious taco experience.

Caribbean Jerk Pork Tacos with Pineapple Salsa

Ingredients:

For the Caribbean Jerk Pork:

- 1.5 pounds pork shoulder or pork tenderloin, thinly sliced
- 3 tablespoons Caribbean jerk seasoning
- 2 tablespoons olive oil
- 2 tablespoons soy sauce
- 1 tablespoon brown sugar
- 1 tablespoon lime juice
- 2 cloves garlic, minced
- 1 teaspoon thyme, dried
- 1 teaspoon allspice
- Salt and black pepper to taste

For the Pineapple Salsa:

- 1 cup fresh pineapple, diced
- 1/2 red onion, finely chopped
- 1 jalapeño, seeds removed and finely chopped
- 1/4 cup fresh cilantro, chopped
- Juice of 1 lime
- Salt and black pepper to taste

For Tacos:

- Small corn or flour tortillas
- Shredded cabbage or lettuce
- Avocado slices
- Lime wedges for serving

Instructions:

1. Prepare Caribbean Jerk Pork:

   In a bowl, combine Caribbean jerk seasoning, olive oil, soy sauce, brown sugar, lime juice, minced garlic, dried thyme, allspice, salt, and black pepper.
   Add thinly sliced pork to the marinade, ensuring it's well coated. Allow it to marinate for at least 30 minutes.

Heat a skillet or grill over medium-high heat. Cook the marinated pork slices until browned and cooked through.

2. Prepare Pineapple Salsa:

   In a bowl, combine diced pineapple, finely chopped red onion, chopped jalapeño, chopped cilantro, lime juice, salt, and black pepper.
   Mix well and set aside.

3. Assemble Tacos:

   Warm tortillas according to package instructions.
   Spoon shredded cabbage or lettuce onto each tortilla.
   Top with Caribbean Jerk Pork.
   Add avocado slices.
   Spoon Pineapple Salsa over the filling.
   Serve with lime wedges on the side.

4. Serve:

Enjoy your Caribbean Jerk Pork Tacos with Pineapple Salsa immediately. The combination of the spicy jerk pork and the sweet-tangy pineapple salsa creates a delicious and flavorful taco experience with a tropical twist.

Turkish Lamb Kofta Tacos with Cucumber Yogurt Sauce

Ingredients:

For the Lamb Kofta:

- 1.5 pounds ground lamb
- 1 onion, finely grated
- 3 cloves garlic, minced
- 2 tablespoons fresh parsley, chopped
- 1 teaspoon ground cumin
- 1 teaspoon ground coriander
- 1 teaspoon paprika
- 1/2 teaspoon cayenne pepper (adjust to taste)
- Salt and black pepper to taste
- Olive oil for cooking

For the Cucumber Yogurt Sauce:

- 1 cup Greek yogurt
- 1 cucumber, grated and squeezed to remove excess water
- 2 tablespoons fresh mint, chopped
- 1 tablespoon fresh dill, chopped
- 1 tablespoon lemon juice
- Salt and black pepper to taste

For Tacos:

- Small flatbreads or tortillas
- Sliced red onions
- Fresh tomatoes, diced
- Fresh mint leaves for garnish
- Lemon wedges for serving

Instructions:

1. Prepare Lamb Kofta:

    In a bowl, combine ground lamb, finely grated onion, minced garlic, chopped fresh parsley, ground cumin, ground coriander, paprika, cayenne pepper, salt, and black pepper. Mix the ingredients thoroughly and shape the mixture into small cylindrical kofta (kebab) shapes.

Heat olive oil in a skillet over medium-high heat. Cook the lamb kofta until browned on all sides and cooked through.

2. Prepare Cucumber Yogurt Sauce:

In a bowl, combine Greek yogurt, grated cucumber, chopped fresh mint, chopped fresh dill, lemon juice, salt, and black pepper.
Mix well and refrigerate until ready to use.

3. Assemble Tacos:

Warm flatbreads or tortillas according to package instructions.
Spread a generous layer of Cucumber Yogurt Sauce onto each flatbread.
Place a few Lamb Kofta on top of the sauce.
Add sliced red onions and diced tomatoes.
Garnish with fresh mint leaves.
Serve with lemon wedges on the side.

4. Serve:

Enjoy your Turkish Lamb Kofta Tacos with Cucumber Yogurt Sauce immediately. The combination of the flavorful lamb kofta and the cooling cucumber yogurt sauce creates a delicious and satisfying taco experience with Turkish flair.

Vietnamese Banh Mi Tacos with Pickled Daikon and Carrots

Ingredients:

For the Banh Mi Tacos:

- 1 pound boneless pork shoulder or pork tenderloin, thinly sliced
- 2 tablespoons soy sauce
- 2 tablespoons fish sauce
- 2 tablespoons sugar
- 1 tablespoon vegetable oil
- 2 cloves garlic, minced
- 1 teaspoon five-spice powder
- 1 teaspoon black pepper
- Corn or flour tortillas

For the Pickled Daikon and Carrots:

- 1 cup julienned daikon radish
- 1 cup julienned carrots
- 1/2 cup rice vinegar
- 1/4 cup sugar
- 1/2 teaspoon salt

For the Cucumber Yogurt Sauce:

- 1 cup Greek yogurt
- 1 cucumber, finely diced
- 2 tablespoons fresh mint, chopped
- 1 tablespoon lime juice
- Salt and black pepper to taste

Toppings and Garnishes:

- Fresh cilantro leaves
- Sliced jalapeños
- Sliced cucumbers
- Sliced radishes
- Sriracha sauce (optional)

Instructions:

1. Prepare Pickled Daikon and Carrots:

    In a bowl, combine julienned daikon radish and carrots.
    In a separate bowl, mix rice vinegar, sugar, and salt until the sugar and salt dissolve.
    Pour the vinegar mixture over the daikon and carrots, ensuring they are well coated. Let it marinate for at least 30 minutes.

2. Prepare Cucumber Yogurt Sauce:

    In a bowl, combine Greek yogurt, finely diced cucumber, chopped fresh mint, lime juice, salt, and black pepper.
    Mix well and refrigerate until ready to use.

3. Prepare Banh Mi Tacos:

    In a bowl, whisk together soy sauce, fish sauce, sugar, vegetable oil, minced garlic, five-spice powder, and black pepper.
    Add thinly sliced pork to the marinade, ensuring it's well coated. Allow it to marinate for at least 30 minutes.
    Cook the marinated pork in a skillet over medium-high heat until browned and cooked through.

4. Assemble Tacos:

    Warm tortillas according to package instructions.
    Spoon the cooked pork onto each tortilla.
    Top with pickled daikon and carrots.
    Drizzle with cucumber yogurt sauce.
    Garnish with fresh cilantro leaves, sliced jalapeños, sliced cucumbers, and sliced radishes.
    Optionally, add a drizzle of Sriracha for extra heat.

5. Serve:

Enjoy your Vietnamese Banh Mi Tacos with Pickled Daikon and Carrots immediately. The combination of the savory pork, tangy pickled vegetables, and refreshing cucumber yogurt sauce creates a delightful and flavorful taco experience.

Greek Souvlaki Tacos with Tzatziki and Feta

Ingredients:

For the Souvlaki:

- 1.5 pounds boneless, skinless chicken thighs or lamb, cut into bite-sized pieces
- 1/4 cup olive oil
- 3 tablespoons red wine vinegar
- 2 teaspoons dried oregano
- 1 teaspoon dried thyme
- 1 teaspoon garlic powder
- Salt and black pepper to taste
- Tzatziki sauce (store-bought or homemade, see below)

For the Tzatziki Sauce:

- 1 cup Greek yogurt
- 1 cucumber, grated and drained
- 2 cloves garlic, minced
- 1 tablespoon fresh dill, chopped
- 1 tablespoon olive oil
- 1 tablespoon lemon juice
- Salt and black pepper to taste

For Tacos:

- Small corn or flour tortillas
- Crumbled feta cheese
- Sliced red onions
- Cherry tomatoes, halved
- Kalamata olives, sliced
- Fresh parsley, chopped (for garnish)
- Lemon wedges for serving

Instructions:

1. Prepare Souvlaki:

>In a bowl, whisk together olive oil, red wine vinegar, dried oregano, dried thyme, garlic powder, salt, and black pepper.

Add the bite-sized chicken or lamb pieces to the marinade, ensuring they are well coated. Marinate for at least 30 minutes.

Cook the marinated meat in a skillet or grill over medium-high heat until fully cooked and slightly charred.

2. Prepare Tzatziki Sauce:

In a bowl, combine Greek yogurt, grated and drained cucumber, minced garlic, chopped fresh dill, olive oil, lemon juice, salt, and black pepper.

Mix well and refrigerate until ready to use.

3. Assemble Tacos:

Warm tortillas according to package instructions.

Spoon the cooked souvlaki onto each tortilla.

Drizzle with Tzatziki sauce.

Top with crumbled feta cheese, sliced red onions, halved cherry tomatoes, and sliced Kalamata olives.

Garnish with fresh parsley.

Serve with lemon wedges on the side.

4. Serve:

Enjoy your Greek Souvlaki Tacos with Tzatziki and Feta immediately. The combination of the juicy souvlaki, creamy tzatziki, and the bold flavors of feta and Mediterranean toppings create a delicious and satisfying taco experience.

Argentinian Chimichurri Steak Tacos with Grilled Corn Salsa

Ingredients:

For the Chimichurri Steak:

- 1.5 pounds flank steak or skirt steak
- 1 cup fresh parsley, finely chopped
- 1/4 cup fresh cilantro, finely chopped
- 4 cloves garlic, minced
- 1/2 cup red wine vinegar
- 1/2 cup olive oil
- 1 teaspoon dried oregano
- 1 teaspoon red pepper flakes (adjust to taste)
- Salt and black pepper to taste

For the Grilled Corn Salsa:

- 2 cups fresh corn kernels (about 4 ears of corn)
- 1 red bell pepper, diced
- 1/2 red onion, finely chopped
- 1 jalapeño, seeds removed and finely chopped
- Juice of 1 lime
- 2 tablespoons fresh cilantro, chopped
- Salt and black pepper to taste

For Tacos:

- Small corn or flour tortillas
- Sliced avocado
- Crumbled queso fresco or feta cheese
- Lime wedges for serving

Instructions:

1. Prepare Chimichurri Steak:

   In a bowl, combine finely chopped parsley, minced garlic, red wine vinegar, olive oil, dried oregano, red pepper flakes, salt, and black pepper to create the chimichurri sauce. Reserve a portion of the chimichurri sauce for serving and use the rest to marinate the steak. Allow the steak to marinate for at least 30 minutes.

Grill the marinated steak to your desired doneness. Allow it to rest for a few minutes before slicing.

2. Prepare Grilled Corn Salsa:

Grill corn on the cob until slightly charred. Cut the kernels off the cob.
In a bowl, combine grilled corn kernels, diced red bell pepper, finely chopped red onion, chopped jalapeño, lime juice, chopped cilantro, salt, and black pepper. Mix well.

3. Assemble Tacos:

Warm tortillas according to package instructions.
Slice the chimichurri-marinated steak.
Place slices of steak onto each tortilla.
Top with grilled corn salsa.
Add sliced avocado and crumbled queso fresco or feta cheese.
Drizzle with reserved chimichurri sauce.
Serve with lime wedges on the side.

4. Serve:

Enjoy your Argentinian Chimichurri Steak Tacos with Grilled Corn Salsa immediately. The combination of the herby chimichurri, grilled steak, and sweet corn salsa creates a delicious and satisfying taco experience with Argentinian flair.

Thai Green Curry Vegetable Tacos with Peanut Sauce

Ingredients:

For the Thai Green Curry Vegetables:

- 1 tablespoon green curry paste
- 1 can (14 oz) coconut milk
- 2 tablespoons soy sauce
- 1 tablespoon brown sugar
- 1 tablespoon vegetable oil
- 1 onion, thinly sliced
- 1 bell pepper (any color), thinly sliced
- 1 zucchini, thinly sliced
- 1 cup broccoli florets
- 1 carrot, julienned
- 1 cup snap peas, ends trimmed
- Fresh cilantro, chopped (for garnish)

For the Peanut Sauce:

- 1/2 cup creamy peanut butter
- 2 tablespoons soy sauce
- 2 tablespoons rice vinegar
- 1 tablespoon sesame oil
- 1 tablespoon honey or agave nectar
- 1 clove garlic, minced
- 1 teaspoon grated ginger
- Water (as needed to adjust consistency)

For Tacos:

- Small corn or flour tortillas
- Cooked jasmine rice
- Bean sprouts
- Lime wedges for serving

Instructions:

1. Prepare Thai Green Curry Vegetables:

In a bowl, mix green curry paste, coconut milk, soy sauce, and brown sugar. Set aside.

Heat vegetable oil in a large skillet over medium heat. Add sliced onion and cook until softened.

Add bell pepper, zucchini, broccoli, carrot, and snap peas to the skillet. Stir-fry for a few minutes until the vegetables are slightly tender.

Pour the green curry mixture over the vegetables. Simmer for 5-7 minutes until the vegetables are cooked but still vibrant.

Garnish with chopped fresh cilantro.

2. Prepare Peanut Sauce:

In a bowl, whisk together peanut butter, soy sauce, rice vinegar, sesame oil, honey or agave nectar, minced garlic, and grated ginger.

Adjust the consistency with water as needed. Set aside.

3. Assemble Tacos:

Warm tortillas according to package instructions.
Spoon cooked jasmine rice onto each tortilla.
Top with Thai Green Curry Vegetables.
Drizzle with Peanut Sauce.
Add a handful of bean sprouts on top.
Serve with lime wedges on the side.

4. Serve:

Enjoy your Thai Green Curry Vegetable Tacos with Peanut Sauce immediately. The combination of the aromatic green curry vegetables and the rich peanut sauce creates a delicious and exotic taco experience.

Spanish Paella Tacos with Saffron Aioli

Ingredients:

For the Paella Filling:

- 1 cup Arborio rice
- 1/2 pound chicken thighs, boneless and skinless, diced
- 1/2 pound shrimp, peeled and deveined
- 1/2 pound chorizo sausage, sliced
- 1 onion, finely chopped
- 3 cloves garlic, minced
- 1 red bell pepper, diced
- 1 cup frozen peas
- 1 teaspoon smoked paprika
- 1/2 teaspoon saffron threads
- 2 1/2 cups chicken broth
- 1/2 cup dry white wine
- Salt and black pepper to taste
- Olive oil for cooking

For the Saffron Aioli:

- 1/2 cup mayonnaise
- 1 clove garlic, minced
- 1/2 teaspoon saffron threads, crushed
- 1 tablespoon lemon juice
- Salt and black pepper to taste

For Tacos:

- Small corn or flour tortillas
- Lemon wedges for serving
- Fresh parsley, chopped (for garnish)

Instructions:

1. Prepare Paella Filling:

    In a small bowl, soak saffron threads in warm water for about 10 minutes.
    In a paella pan or large skillet, heat olive oil over medium heat.

Add diced chicken thighs and cook until browned. Remove from the pan and set aside.
In the same pan, add sliced chorizo and cook until slightly crispy. Remove and set aside.
In the same pan, sauté chopped onion and minced garlic until softened.
Add Arborio rice and smoked paprika, stirring to coat the rice in the flavors.
Pour in the dry white wine, scraping any browned bits from the bottom of the pan.
Add chicken broth, soaked saffron threads (along with the water), diced bell pepper, and frozen peas. Stir well.
Return the cooked chicken and chorizo to the pan. Simmer until the rice is cooked and the liquid is absorbed.
Add shrimp to the pan and cook until they turn pink and opaque.
Season with salt and black pepper to taste.

2. Prepare Saffron Aioli:

In a small bowl, combine mayonnaise, minced garlic, crushed saffron threads, lemon juice, salt, and black pepper.
Mix well and refrigerate until ready to use.

3. Assemble Tacos:

Warm tortillas according to package instructions.
Spoon the paella filling onto each tortilla.
Drizzle with saffron aioli.
Garnish with chopped fresh parsley.
Serve with lemon wedges on the side.

4. Serve:

Enjoy your Spanish Paella Tacos with Saffron Aioli immediately. The combination of the saffron-infused paella filling and the flavorful saffron aioli creates a unique and delicious taco experience with Spanish flair.

African Peri-Peri Chicken Tacos with Mango Avocado Relish

Ingredients:

For the Peri-Peri Chicken:

- 1.5 pounds chicken thighs, boneless and skinless
- 1/4 cup peri-peri sauce (store-bought or homemade)
- 2 tablespoons olive oil
- 2 cloves garlic, minced
- 1 teaspoon paprika
- 1 teaspoon dried oregano
- Salt and black pepper to taste

For the Mango Avocado Relish:

- 1 ripe mango, diced
- 1 avocado, diced
- 1/4 cup red onion, finely chopped
- 1/4 cup fresh cilantro, chopped
- Juice of 1 lime
- Salt and black pepper to taste

For Tacos:

- Small corn or flour tortillas
- Shredded lettuce or cabbage
- Sliced radishes
- Fresh cilantro leaves
- Lime wedges for serving

Instructions:

1. Prepare Peri-Peri Chicken:

>In a bowl, whisk together peri-peri sauce, olive oil, minced garlic, paprika, dried oregano, salt, and black pepper.
>Add chicken thighs to the marinade, ensuring they are well coated. Allow them to marinate for at least 30 minutes.
>Grill or cook the marinated chicken thighs until fully cooked and slightly charred.

2. Prepare Mango Avocado Relish:

   In a bowl, combine diced mango, diced avocado, finely chopped red onion, chopped fresh cilantro, lime juice, salt, and black pepper.
   Mix well and set aside.

3. Assemble Tacos:

   Warm tortillas according to package instructions.
   Shred the cooked peri-peri chicken.
   Place shredded lettuce or cabbage onto each tortilla.
   Top with the shredded peri-peri chicken.
   Spoon mango avocado relish over the chicken.
   Garnish with sliced radishes and fresh cilantro leaves.
   Serve with lime wedges on the side.

4. Serve:

Enjoy your African Peri-Peri Chicken Tacos with Mango Avocado Relish immediately. The combination of the spicy peri-peri chicken and the sweet and tangy mango avocado relish creates a unique and delicious taco experience with African-inspired flavors.

Irish Corned Beef and Cabbage Tacos with Mustard Sauce

Ingredients:

For the Corned Beef and Cabbage:

- 1 pound corned beef, cooked and shredded
- 2 cups green cabbage, finely shredded
- 1 onion, thinly sliced
- 2 cloves garlic, minced
- 1 tablespoon vegetable oil
- Salt and black pepper to taste

For the Mustard Sauce:

- 1/2 cup mayonnaise
- 2 tablespoons Dijon mustard
- 1 tablespoon whole grain mustard
- 1 tablespoon honey
- 1 tablespoon apple cider vinegar
- Salt and black pepper to taste

For Tacos:

- Small corn or flour tortillas
- Sliced radishes
- Fresh parsley or cilantro, chopped (for garnish)
- Lemon wedges for serving

Instructions:

1. Prepare Corned Beef and Cabbage:

    Heat vegetable oil in a skillet over medium heat.
    Add thinly sliced onions and cook until softened.
    Add minced garlic and shredded cabbage to the skillet. Sauté until the cabbage is tender.
    Stir in shredded corned beef and cook until heated through.
    Season with salt and black pepper to taste.

2. Prepare Mustard Sauce:

In a bowl, whisk together mayonnaise, Dijon mustard, whole grain mustard, honey, apple cider vinegar, salt, and black pepper.
Adjust the seasoning according to your taste. Set aside.

3. Assemble Tacos:

Warm tortillas according to package instructions.
Spoon the corned beef and cabbage mixture onto each tortilla.
Drizzle with mustard sauce.
Garnish with sliced radishes and chopped fresh parsley or cilantro.
Serve with lemon wedges on the side.

4. Serve:

Enjoy your Irish Corned Beef and Cabbage Tacos with Mustard Sauce immediately. The combination of the tender corned beef, sautéed cabbage, and zesty mustard sauce creates a delicious and unique taco experience with Irish inspiration.

Indonesian Satay Chicken Tacos with Peanut Drizzle

Ingredients:

For the Satay Chicken:

- 1 pound boneless, skinless chicken thighs, thinly sliced
- 1/4 cup soy sauce
- 2 tablespoons kecap manis (sweet soy sauce)
- 2 tablespoons peanut butter
- 2 cloves garlic, minced
- 1 teaspoon ground coriander
- 1 teaspoon ground cumin
- 1 teaspoon turmeric powder
- 1 tablespoon vegetable oil
- Bamboo skewers, soaked in water

For the Peanut Drizzle:

- 1/3 cup creamy peanut butter
- 2 tablespoons soy sauce
- 1 tablespoon honey
- 1 tablespoon rice vinegar
- 1 teaspoon sesame oil
- Water (as needed to adjust consistency)

For Tacos:

- Small corn or flour tortillas
- Shredded cabbage or lettuce
- Sliced cucumber
- Fresh cilantro leaves
- Crushed peanuts (for garnish)
- Lime wedges for serving

Instructions:

1. Prepare Satay Chicken:

    In a bowl, whisk together soy sauce, kecap manis, peanut butter, minced garlic, ground coriander, ground cumin, turmeric powder, and vegetable oil.

Add thinly sliced chicken to the marinade, ensuring it's well coated. Marinate for at least 30 minutes.

Thread marinated chicken onto soaked bamboo skewers.

Grill or cook the skewers until the chicken is cooked through and has a nice char.

2. Prepare Peanut Drizzle:

In a bowl, whisk together peanut butter, soy sauce, honey, rice vinegar, and sesame oil.

Adjust the consistency with water as needed. Set aside.

3. Assemble Tacos:

Warm tortillas according to package instructions.

Arrange shredded cabbage or lettuce on each tortilla.

Place slices of grilled satay chicken on top.

Add sliced cucumber.

Drizzle with peanut sauce.

Garnish with fresh cilantro leaves and crushed peanuts.

Serve with lime wedges on the side.

4. Serve:

Enjoy your Indonesian Satay Chicken Tacos with Peanut Drizzle immediately. The combination of the flavorful satay chicken and the rich peanut drizzle creates a delicious and exotic taco experience with Indonesian flair.

Lebanese Shawarma Tacos with Garlic Tahini Sauce

Ingredients:

For the Shawarma:

- 1 pound boneless chicken thighs, thinly sliced (or beef or lamb)
- 3 cloves garlic, minced
- 2 teaspoons ground cumin
- 2 teaspoons ground coriander
- 1 teaspoon ground paprika
- 1 teaspoon ground turmeric
- 1 teaspoon ground cinnamon
- 1 teaspoon ground allspice
- 1/4 teaspoon cayenne pepper
- 1/4 cup plain yogurt
- 2 tablespoons olive oil
- Salt and black pepper to taste

For the Garlic Tahini Sauce:

- 1/2 cup tahini
- 2 tablespoons olive oil
- 2 cloves garlic, minced
- 2 tablespoons lemon juice
- 1/2 teaspoon ground cumin
- Salt and black pepper to taste
- Water (as needed to adjust consistency)

For Tacos:

- Small corn or flour tortillas
- Sliced tomatoes
- Sliced cucumbers
- Chopped fresh parsley
- Pickled turnips or radishes (optional)
- Lemon wedges for serving

Instructions:

1. Prepare Shawarma:

In a bowl, combine minced garlic, ground cumin, ground coriander, ground paprika, ground turmeric, ground cinnamon, ground allspice, cayenne pepper, plain yogurt, olive oil, salt, and black pepper.

Add thinly sliced chicken thighs to the marinade, ensuring they are well coated. Marinate for at least 1-2 hours or overnight.

Cook the marinated chicken in a skillet over medium-high heat until fully cooked and slightly charred.

2. Prepare Garlic Tahini Sauce:

In a bowl, whisk together tahini, olive oil, minced garlic, lemon juice, ground cumin, salt, and black pepper.

Adjust the consistency with water as needed. Set aside.

3. Assemble Tacos:

Warm tortillas according to package instructions.
Spoon the cooked shawarma onto each tortilla.
Add sliced tomatoes and cucumbers.
Drizzle with garlic tahini sauce.
Garnish with chopped fresh parsley.
Optionally, add pickled turnips or radishes for extra flavor.
Serve with lemon wedges on the side.

4. Serve:

Enjoy your Lebanese Shawarma Tacos with Garlic Tahini Sauce immediately. The combination of the spiced shawarma and the creamy tahini sauce creates a delicious and satisfying taco experience with Lebanese flair.

Mexican Mole Chicken Tacos with Sesame Seeds

Ingredients:

For the Mole Chicken:

- 1.5 pounds boneless, skinless chicken thighs
- 2 tablespoons vegetable oil
- 1 onion, chopped
- 3 cloves garlic, minced
- 2 dried ancho chilies, stemmed and seeded
- 2 dried guajillo chilies, stemmed and seeded
- 2 tomatoes, chopped
- 1/4 cup raisins
- 2 tablespoons almonds
- 2 tablespoons sesame seeds, plus extra for garnish
- 1/4 teaspoon ground cinnamon
- 1/4 teaspoon ground cumin
- 1/4 teaspoon dried oregano
- 3 cups chicken broth
- Salt and black pepper to taste

For Tacos:

- Small corn or flour tortillas
- Shredded lettuce or cabbage
- Sliced radishes
- Chopped fresh cilantro
- Lime wedges for serving

Instructions:

1. Prepare Mole Chicken:

   In a large skillet, heat vegetable oil over medium heat.
   Add chopped onions and minced garlic, sauté until softened.
   Add dried ancho chilies, guajillo chilies, tomatoes, raisins, almonds, sesame seeds, ground cinnamon, ground cumin, and dried oregano to the skillet. Cook for about 5 minutes until the ingredients are slightly toasted.
   Transfer the mixture to a blender. Add chicken broth and blend until smooth.
   In the same skillet, brown chicken thighs on both sides.

Pour the mole sauce over the chicken, reduce heat, and simmer for 25-30 minutes until the chicken is cooked through and the sauce has thickened. Season with salt and black pepper to taste.

2. Assemble Tacos:

Warm tortillas according to package instructions.
Shred the mole chicken.
Place shredded lettuce or cabbage onto each tortilla.
Top with the shredded mole chicken.
Add sliced radishes and chopped fresh cilantro.
Drizzle with extra mole sauce from the skillet.
Garnish with sesame seeds.

3. Serve:

Enjoy your Mexican Mole Chicken Tacos with Sesame Seeds immediately. The rich and savory mole sauce combined with the nutty sesame seeds creates a delicious and unique taco experience with Mexican flair.

Italian Caprese Tacos with Balsamic Glaze

Ingredients:

For the Caprese Filling:

- 1 pint cherry tomatoes, halved
- 8 oz fresh mozzarella, diced
- Fresh basil leaves, torn
- Balsamic glaze for drizzling
- Salt and black pepper to taste

For Balsamic Glaze:

- 1/2 cup balsamic vinegar
- 2 tablespoons honey or maple syrup

For Tacos:

- Small flour or corn tortillas
- Extra virgin olive oil
- Balsamic glaze for drizzling
- Fresh basil leaves for garnish

Instructions:

1. Prepare Balsamic Glaze:

    In a small saucepan, combine balsamic vinegar and honey or maple syrup.
    Bring to a simmer over medium heat, then reduce the heat to low.
    Simmer for about 10-15 minutes or until the mixture has thickened and coats the back of a spoon.
    Remove from heat and let it cool. The glaze will continue to thicken as it cools.

2. Prepare Caprese Filling:

    In a bowl, combine halved cherry tomatoes, diced fresh mozzarella, and torn fresh basil leaves.
    Drizzle with balsamic glaze and gently toss until well combined.
    Season with salt and black pepper to taste.

3. Assemble Tacos:

Warm tortillas in a dry skillet or oven according to package instructions.
Lightly brush each tortilla with extra virgin olive oil.
Spoon the Caprese filling onto each tortilla.
Drizzle with balsamic glaze.
Garnish with fresh basil leaves.

4. Serve:

Enjoy your Italian Caprese Tacos with Balsamic Glaze immediately. The combination of juicy tomatoes, creamy mozzarella, and fragrant basil, all drizzled with sweet balsamic glaze, creates a fresh and delightful taco experience with Italian flair.

Cuban Ropa Vieja Tacos with Plantain Chips

Ingredients:

For the Ropa Vieja:

- 2 pounds flank steak or skirt steak
- 1 large onion, sliced
- 1 bell pepper (any color), sliced
- 3 cloves garlic, minced
- 1 can (14 oz) crushed tomatoes
- 1 cup beef broth
- 1/2 cup dry white wine (optional)
- 2 teaspoons ground cumin
- 1 teaspoon dried oregano
- 1 teaspoon smoked paprika
- Salt and black pepper to taste
- Olive oil for cooking

For Plantain Chips:

- 2 large green plantains, thinly sliced
- Vegetable oil for frying
- Salt to taste

For Tacos:

- Small corn or flour tortillas
- Shredded lettuce or cabbage
- Diced tomatoes
- Sliced red onions
- Fresh cilantro, chopped
- Lime wedges for serving

Instructions:

1. Prepare Ropa Vieja:

   Season the steak with salt, black pepper, ground cumin, dried oregano, and smoked paprika.
   In a large skillet or Dutch oven, heat olive oil over medium-high heat.
   Brown the seasoned steak on both sides, then remove and set aside.

In the same skillet, sauté sliced onions, sliced bell peppers, and minced garlic until softened.

Pour in crushed tomatoes, beef broth, and white wine (if using). Stir to combine.

Return the browned steak to the skillet, ensuring it's submerged in the sauce.

Cover and simmer for 2-3 hours or until the meat easily shreds with a fork.

Shred the beef with two forks and cook uncovered for an additional 15-20 minutes until the sauce thickens.

2. Prepare Plantain Chips:

Peel the plantains and thinly slice them diagonally.

In a large skillet, heat vegetable oil over medium heat.

Fry the plantain slices until golden brown and crispy. Remove and drain on paper towels.

Season with salt to taste.

3. Assemble Tacos:

Warm tortillas according to package instructions.

Place shredded lettuce or cabbage onto each tortilla.

Spoon Ropa Vieja onto the lettuce.

Top with diced tomatoes, sliced red onions, and chopped fresh cilantro.

Add a handful of crispy plantain chips on top.

Serve with lime wedges on the side.

4. Serve:

Enjoy your Cuban Ropa Vieja Tacos with Plantain Chips immediately. The combination of the flavorful shredded beef and the crunchy plantain chips creates a delicious and satisfying taco experience with Cuban flair.

Filipino Adobo Pork Tacos with Pineapple Salsa

Ingredients:

For the Adobo Pork:

- 1.5 pounds pork shoulder, cut into bite-sized pieces
- 1/2 cup soy sauce
- 1/4 cup white vinegar
- 1/4 cup water
- 3 cloves garlic, minced
- 1 bay leaf
- 1 teaspoon peppercorns
- 2 tablespoons vegetable oil

For Pineapple Salsa:

- 1 cup fresh pineapple, diced
- 1/2 red onion, finely chopped
- 1 jalapeño, seeds removed and finely chopped
- 1/4 cup fresh cilantro, chopped
- Juice of 1 lime
- Salt to taste

For Tacos:

- Small corn or flour tortillas
- Shredded green cabbage or lettuce
- Crumbled queso fresco or feta cheese
- Lime wedges for serving

Instructions:

1. Prepare Adobo Pork:

   In a bowl, combine soy sauce, white vinegar, water, minced garlic, bay leaf, and peppercorns to create the Adobo marinade.
   Add the bite-sized pork pieces to the marinade, ensuring they are well coated. Marinate for at least 30 minutes.
   In a large skillet, heat vegetable oil over medium-high heat.
   Add the marinated pork and cook until browned on all sides.

Pour the remaining marinade into the skillet, reduce heat, cover, and simmer for 30-40 minutes or until the pork is tender and the sauce has thickened.

2. Prepare Pineapple Salsa:

In a bowl, combine diced fresh pineapple, finely chopped red onion, chopped jalapeño, chopped cilantro, lime juice, and salt to taste.
Mix well and set aside.

3. Assemble Tacos:

Warm tortillas according to package instructions.
Place shredded green cabbage or lettuce onto each tortilla.
Spoon the Adobo pork onto the cabbage or lettuce.
Top with pineapple salsa.
Sprinkle crumbled queso fresco or feta cheese on top.
Serve with lime wedges on the side.

4. Serve:

Enjoy your Filipino Adobo Pork Tacos with Pineapple Salsa immediately. The combination of the savory Adobo pork and the sweet-and-tangy pineapple salsa creates a delicious and unique taco experience with Filipino flavors.

Swedish Swedish Meatball Tacos with Lingonberry Sauce

Ingredients:

For the Swedish Meatballs:

- 1 pound ground beef
- 1/2 pound ground pork
- 1/2 cup breadcrumbs
- 1/2 cup milk
- 1 small onion, finely chopped
- 2 cloves garlic, minced
- 1 egg
- 1 teaspoon salt
- 1/2 teaspoon black pepper
- 1/4 teaspoon ground allspice
- 1/4 teaspoon ground nutmeg
- Butter or oil for cooking

For the Lingonberry Sauce:

- 1 cup lingonberry preserves or cranberry sauce
- 2 tablespoons water
- 1 tablespoon honey or maple syrup

For Tacos:

- Small flour or corn tortillas
- Sour cream or Greek yogurt
- Chopped fresh parsley or dill for garnish
- Pickled cucumbers (optional)
- Lingonberry sauce for drizzling

Instructions:

1. Prepare Swedish Meatballs:

   In a bowl, combine breadcrumbs and milk. Let it sit for a few minutes.
   In a large mixing bowl, add ground beef, ground pork, soaked breadcrumbs, chopped onion, minced garlic, egg, salt, black pepper, allspice, and nutmeg.
   Mix the ingredients until well combined.
   Form the mixture into small meatballs.

In a skillet, heat butter or oil over medium heat. Cook the meatballs until browned on all sides and cooked through.

2. Prepare Lingonberry Sauce:

In a small saucepan, combine lingonberry preserves or cranberry sauce, water, and honey or maple syrup.
Heat over low-medium heat, stirring occasionally, until the sauce is warmed through and well combined.

3. Assemble Tacos:

Warm tortillas according to package instructions.
Place a few Swedish meatballs onto each tortilla.
Drizzle with lingonberry sauce.
Add a dollop of sour cream or Greek yogurt.
Garnish with chopped fresh parsley or dill.
Optionally, add pickled cucumbers for extra flavor.

4. Serve:

Enjoy your Swedish Meatball Tacos with Lingonberry Sauce immediately. The combination of the savory meatballs and the sweet-tart lingonberry sauce creates a delightful taco experience with Swedish flair.

Bangladeshi Fish Curry Tacos with Cilantro Yogurt

Ingredients:

For the Fish Curry:

- 1 pound white fish fillets (tilapia, cod, or any firm white fish)
- 1 onion, finely chopped
- 2 tomatoes, chopped
- 3 cloves garlic, minced
- 1-inch ginger, grated
- 1 teaspoon ground turmeric
- 1 teaspoon ground cumin
- 1 teaspoon ground coriander
- 1/2 teaspoon chili powder (adjust to taste)
- 1/2 teaspoon paprika
- 1/2 teaspoon garam masala
- Salt to taste
- 2 tablespoons vegetable oil
- Fresh cilantro, chopped (for garnish)

For Cilantro Yogurt:

- 1 cup plain yogurt
- 1/4 cup fresh cilantro, chopped
- 1 tablespoon lime juice
- Salt to taste

For Tacos:

- Small flour or corn tortillas
- Shredded lettuce or cabbage
- Sliced red onions
- Sliced cucumbers
- Lime wedges for serving

Instructions:

1. Prepare Fish Curry:

In a bowl, mix ground turmeric, ground cumin, ground coriander, chili powder, paprika, garam masala, and salt. This is your spice blend.

Cut the fish fillets into bite-sized pieces and coat them with half of the spice blend.
In a large skillet, heat vegetable oil over medium heat.
Add chopped onions and sauté until softened.
Add minced garlic and grated ginger, cook for another minute.
Add chopped tomatoes and the remaining spice blend. Cook until tomatoes are soft and oil begins to separate.
Gently add the fish pieces to the skillet and coat them with the tomato and spice mixture.
Cover and let it simmer for about 10-15 minutes until the fish is cooked through.
Garnish with chopped fresh cilantro.

2. Prepare Cilantro Yogurt:

In a bowl, combine plain yogurt, chopped cilantro, lime juice, and salt. Mix well and set aside.

3. Assemble Tacos:

Warm tortillas according to package instructions.
Place shredded lettuce or cabbage onto each tortilla.
Spoon the Bangladeshi fish curry onto the lettuce.
Top with sliced red onions and cucumbers.
Drizzle with cilantro yogurt.
Serve with lime wedges on the side.

4. Serve:

Enjoy your Bangladeshi Fish Curry Tacos with Cilantro Yogurt immediately. The combination of the flavorful fish curry and the cooling cilantro yogurt creates a delicious and unique taco experience with Bangladeshi influences.

Australian Grilled Kangaroo Tacos with Bush Tomato Salsa

Ingredients:

For the Grilled Kangaroo:

- 1 pound kangaroo steak, thinly sliced
- 2 tablespoons olive oil
- 2 cloves garlic, minced
- 1 teaspoon ground cumin
- 1 teaspoon smoked paprika
- Salt and black pepper to taste

For the Bush Tomato Salsa:

- 1 cup bush tomatoes, rehydrated and chopped (substitute with cherry tomatoes if bush tomatoes are unavailable)
- 1/2 red onion, finely chopped
- 1/2 red bell pepper, finely chopped
- 1/4 cup fresh cilantro, chopped
- 1 tablespoon lime juice
- 1 tablespoon olive oil
- Salt and black pepper to taste

For Tacos:

- Small flour or corn tortillas
- Shredded lettuce or cabbage
- Sliced radishes
- Avocado slices
- Lime wedges for serving

Instructions:

1. Prepare Grilled Kangaroo:

   In a bowl, mix olive oil, minced garlic, ground cumin, smoked paprika, salt, and black pepper.
   Coat the thinly sliced kangaroo steak with the marinade and let it marinate for at least 30 minutes.
   Grill the marinated kangaroo slices over medium-high heat for about 2-3 minutes on each side or until cooked to your liking.

2. Prepare Bush Tomato Salsa:

　　If using dried bush tomatoes, rehydrate them in warm water according to package instructions. Chop the rehydrated bush tomatoes.
　　In a bowl, combine chopped bush tomatoes (or cherry tomatoes), finely chopped red onion, finely chopped red bell pepper, chopped fresh cilantro, lime juice, olive oil, salt, and black pepper. Mix well.

3. Assemble Tacos:

　　Warm tortillas according to package instructions.
　　Place shredded lettuce or cabbage onto each tortilla.
　　Add slices of grilled kangaroo.
　　Spoon bush tomato salsa over the kangaroo slices.
　　Top with sliced radishes and avocado slices.
　　Serve with lime wedges on the side.

4. Serve:

Enjoy your Australian Grilled Kangaroo Tacos with Bush Tomato Salsa immediately. The unique flavors of kangaroo meat paired with the bush tomato salsa create a distinctive and delicious taco experience with Australian flair.

Russian Beef Stroganoff Tacos with Sour Cream and Dill

Ingredients:

For the Beef Stroganoff:

- 1 pound beef sirloin or tenderloin, thinly sliced
- 1 onion, thinly sliced
- 2 tablespoons butter
- 2 tablespoons vegetable oil
- 3 tablespoons all-purpose flour
- 1 cup beef broth
- 2 tablespoons Dijon mustard
- 2 tablespoons Worcestershire sauce
- 1/2 cup sour cream
- Salt and black pepper to taste
- Fresh dill, chopped (for garnish)

For Tacos:

- Small flour or corn tortillas
- Shredded lettuce or cabbage
- Sliced pickles
- Sour cream
- Fresh dill, chopped (for garnish)

Instructions:

1. Prepare Beef Stroganoff:

   In a large skillet, heat butter and vegetable oil over medium-high heat.
   Add thinly sliced beef and cook until browned on all sides. Remove from the skillet and set aside.
   In the same skillet, add thinly sliced onions and cook until softened.
   Sprinkle flour over the onions and stir to create a roux.
   Gradually whisk in beef broth, Dijon mustard, and Worcestershire sauce. Cook until the mixture thickens.
   Add the cooked beef back to the skillet and simmer for a few minutes.
   Stir in sour cream and season with salt and black pepper. Cook until heated through.
   Garnish with chopped fresh dill.

2. Assemble Tacos:

   Warm tortillas according to package instructions.

Place shredded lettuce or cabbage onto each tortilla.
Spoon the beef stroganoff onto the lettuce.
Top with sliced pickles.
Add a dollop of sour cream.
Garnish with additional chopped fresh dill.

3. Serve:

Enjoy your Russian Beef Stroganoff Tacos with Sour Cream and Dill immediately. The combination of the creamy beef stroganoff and the bright flavors of sour cream and dill create a delicious and unique taco experience with Russian influences.

Israeli Falafel Tacos with Hummus and Pickled Radishes

Ingredients:

For the Falafel:

- 1 can (15 oz) chickpeas, drained and rinsed
- 1/2 cup fresh parsley, chopped
- 1/2 cup fresh cilantro, chopped
- 1 small onion, chopped
- 3 cloves garlic, minced
- 1 teaspoon ground cumin
- 1 teaspoon ground coriander
- 1/2 teaspoon baking soda
- Salt and black pepper to taste
- 2-3 tablespoons all-purpose flour (if needed)
- Vegetable oil for frying

For Pickled Radishes:

- 1 bunch radishes, thinly sliced
- 1/2 cup white vinegar
- 1/2 cup water
- 2 tablespoons sugar
- 1 tablespoon salt

For Tacos:

- Small flour or corn tortillas
- Hummus (store-bought or homemade)
- Shredded lettuce or cabbage
- Diced tomatoes
- Tahini sauce for drizzling
- Fresh parsley, chopped (for garnish)
- Sesame seeds (optional, for garnish)
- Lemon wedges for serving

Instructions:

1. Prepare Falafel:

   In a food processor, combine chickpeas, parsley, cilantro, chopped onion, minced garlic, ground cumin, ground coriander, baking soda, salt, and black pepper.
   Pulse the mixture until well combined but still slightly chunky.
   If the mixture is too wet, add flour a tablespoon at a time until it's firm enough to shape into balls.

Form the mixture into small falafel balls.
In a skillet, heat vegetable oil over medium heat.
Fry the falafel balls until golden brown on all sides. Remove and drain on paper towels.

2. Prepare Pickled Radishes:

In a bowl, whisk together white vinegar, water, sugar, and salt until the sugar and salt dissolve.
Place thinly sliced radishes in a jar and pour the vinegar mixture over them.
Let it sit for at least 30 minutes before using.

3. Assemble Tacos:

Warm tortillas according to package instructions.
Spread a spoonful of hummus onto each tortilla.
Place shredded lettuce or cabbage on top of the hummus.
Add a few falafel balls.
Top with diced tomatoes and pickled radishes.
Drizzle with tahini sauce.
Garnish with chopped fresh parsley and sesame seeds if desired.
Serve with lemon wedges on the side.

4. Serve:

Enjoy your Israeli Falafel Tacos with Hummus and Pickled Radishes immediately. The combination of crispy falafel, creamy hummus, and tangy pickled radishes creates a delicious and unique taco experience with Israeli flair.

Canadian Poutine Tacos with Gravy and Cheese Curds

Ingredients:

For the Poutine Filling:

- 1 pound frozen French fries, cooked according to package instructions
- 1 cup cheese curds (preferably fresh and squeaky)
- 1 cup beef or chicken gravy, hot

For Tacos:

- Small flour or corn tortillas
- Fresh chives, chopped (for garnish)

Instructions:

1. Prepare Poutine Filling:

   Cook the frozen French fries according to the package instructions until they are golden and crispy.
   While the fries are still hot, spread them on a serving platter or individual plates.
   Sprinkle cheese curds evenly over the hot fries.

2. Assemble Tacos:

   Warm tortillas according to package instructions.
   Spoon the hot poutine mixture onto each tortilla.
   Drizzle hot beef or chicken gravy over the poutine filling.
   Garnish with fresh chives.

3. Serve:

Enjoy your Canadian Poutine Tacos with Gravy and Cheese Curds immediately. The combination of crispy fries, gooey cheese curds, and savory gravy in a taco format creates a delicious and satisfying fusion of Canadian and Mexican flavors.

Jamaican Jerk Jackfruit Tacos with Mango Salsa

Ingredients:

For the Jamaican Jerk Jackfruit:

- 2 cans (20 oz each) young green jackfruit in water or brine, drained and shredded
- 3 tablespoons Jamaican jerk seasoning
- 2 tablespoons olive oil
- 1 onion, finely chopped
- 3 cloves garlic, minced
- 1 tablespoon soy sauce or tamari
- 1 tablespoon brown sugar
- 1 teaspoon dried thyme
- 1 teaspoon ground allspice
- 1/2 teaspoon cinnamon
- 1/2 teaspoon nutmeg
- Salt and black pepper to taste

For the Mango Salsa:

- 2 ripe mangoes, peeled and diced
- 1/2 red onion, finely chopped
- 1 jalapeño, seeds removed and finely chopped
- 1/4 cup fresh cilantro, chopped
- Juice of 1 lime
- Salt to taste

For Tacos:

- Small flour or corn tortillas
- Shredded cabbage or lettuce
- Avocado slices
- Lime wedges for serving

Instructions:

1. Prepare Jamaican Jerk Jackfruit:

   In a bowl, mix Jamaican jerk seasoning, olive oil, minced garlic, soy sauce, brown sugar, dried thyme, ground allspice, cinnamon, nutmeg, salt, and black pepper to create the jerk marinade.
   Heat a large skillet over medium heat. Add chopped onions and cook until softened.
   Add shredded jackfruit to the skillet and coat it with the jerk marinade. Cook for 5-7 minutes, stirring occasionally.
   Adjust seasoning to taste and cook until the jackfruit is heated through and has absorbed the flavors.

2. Prepare Mango Salsa:

>In a bowl, combine diced mangoes, finely chopped red onion, chopped jalapeño, chopped fresh cilantro, lime juice, and salt. Mix well and set aside.

3. Assemble Tacos:

>Warm tortillas according to package instructions.
>Place shredded cabbage or lettuce onto each tortilla.
>Spoon Jamaican jerk jackfruit onto the cabbage or lettuce.
>Top with avocado slices.
>Spoon mango salsa over the jackfruit.
>Serve with lime wedges on the side.

4. Serve:

Enjoy your Jamaican Jerk Jackfruit Tacos with Mango Salsa immediately. The combination of the spicy and savory jerk jackfruit with the sweet and tangy mango salsa creates a delicious and exotic taco experience.

Chinese Peking Duck Tacos with Hoisin Plum Sauce

Ingredients:

For the Peking Duck:

- 1 Peking duck breast, cooked and shredded (you can find pre-cooked Peking duck at some grocery stores or Chinese markets)
- Hoisin sauce for brushing
- 12 small flour or corn tortillas
- Green onions, thinly sliced (for garnish)
- Sesame seeds (for garnish)

For the Hoisin Plum Sauce:

- 1/4 cup hoisin sauce
- 2 tablespoons plum sauce
- 1 tablespoon soy sauce
- 1 tablespoon rice vinegar
- 1 teaspoon sesame oil
- 1 teaspoon honey
- 1 teaspoon fresh ginger, grated
- 1 clove garlic, minced

Optional Garnishes:

- Shredded Napa cabbage or lettuce
- Thinly sliced cucumber
- Fresh cilantro leaves

Instructions:

1. Prepare Hoisin Plum Sauce:

    In a bowl, whisk together hoisin sauce, plum sauce, soy sauce, rice vinegar, sesame oil, honey, grated ginger, and minced garlic. Set aside.

2. Prepare Peking Duck:

    Cook the Peking duck breast according to package instructions or roast it if it's raw.
    Shred the cooked duck meat.
    Brush the shredded duck meat with hoisin sauce for added flavor.

3. Assemble Tacos:

    Warm tortillas according to package instructions.
    Place a portion of shredded Peking duck onto each tortilla.

> Drizzle hoisin plum sauce over the duck.
> Garnish with thinly sliced green onions and sesame seeds.

4. Optional Garnishes:

> Add shredded Napa cabbage or lettuce for crunch.
> Place thinly sliced cucumber for freshness.
> Sprinkle fresh cilantro leaves for additional flavor.

5. Serve:

Enjoy your Chinese Peking Duck Tacos with Hoisin Plum Sauce immediately. The combination of crispy Peking duck, sweet and savory hoisin plum sauce, and the optional garnishes create a delicious and exotic taco experience with Chinese flair.

Portuguese Bacalhau Tacos with Olive Tapenade

Ingredients:

For the Bacalhau Filling:

- 1 pound salted cod (bacalhau), soaked and shredded
- 1 onion, finely chopped
- 2 cloves garlic, minced
- 2 tablespoons olive oil
- 1 cup cooked potatoes, diced
- 1/4 cup fresh parsley, chopped
- Salt and black pepper to taste

For the Olive Tapenade:

- 1 cup mixed olives, pitted and chopped (green and black)
- 2 tablespoons capers, drained and chopped
- 1 tablespoon fresh parsley, chopped
- 1 tablespoon olive oil
- 1 teaspoon lemon juice
- 1 clove garlic, minced
- Black pepper to taste

For Tacos:

- Small flour or corn tortillas
- Shredded lettuce or cabbage
- Sliced cherry tomatoes
- Lemon wedges for serving

Instructions:

1. Prepare Bacalhau Filling:

   Soak the salted cod (bacalhau) in cold water for 24-48 hours, changing the water every 8 hours.
   Boil the soaked cod until it's cooked through, then shred it into small pieces.
   In a large skillet, heat olive oil over medium heat. Add chopped onions and garlic, sauté until softened.
   Add the shredded bacalhau to the skillet, stirring well with the onions and garlic.
   Add cooked diced potatoes and continue cooking until everything is well combined and heated through.
   Stir in fresh parsley, and season with salt and black pepper to taste.

2. Prepare Olive Tapenade:

In a bowl, combine chopped mixed olives, capers, fresh parsley, olive oil, lemon juice, minced garlic, and black pepper. Mix well.

3. Assemble Tacos:

    Warm tortillas according to package instructions.
    Place shredded lettuce or cabbage onto each tortilla.
    Spoon the bacalhau filling onto the lettuce.
    Top with sliced cherry tomatoes.
    Spoon olive tapenade over the filling.
    Serve with lemon wedges on the side.

4. Serve:

Enjoy your Portuguese Bacalhau Tacos with Olive Tapenade immediately. The combination of the savory bacalhau filling and the briny olive tapenade creates a delicious and unique taco experience with Portuguese influences.

Scottish Haggis Tacos with Neeps and Tatties Mash

Ingredients:

For the Haggis Filling:

- 1 pound haggis (commercially available or homemade)
- 2 tablespoons butter
- 1 onion, finely chopped
- 2 cloves garlic, minced
- 1/4 cup beef or vegetable broth
- Salt and black pepper to taste

For the Neeps and Tatties Mash:

- 2 large potatoes, peeled and diced
- 2 turnips, peeled and diced
- 2 tablespoons butter
- 1/4 cup milk
- Salt and black pepper to taste

For Tacos:

- Small flour or corn tortillas
- Chopped fresh chives or parsley (for garnish)
- Whisky sauce or your favorite hot sauce (optional)

Instructions:

1. Prepare Haggis Filling:

   In a large skillet, melt butter over medium heat. Add chopped onions and garlic, sauté until softened.
   Add haggis to the skillet and break it up with a spoon. Cook until browned.
   Pour in beef or vegetable broth, stirring to combine. Cook for an additional 5 minutes.
   Season with salt and black pepper to taste.

2. Prepare Neeps and Tatties Mash:

   Boil diced potatoes and turnips in a large pot of salted water until tender.
   Drain the water and mash the potatoes and turnips together.
   Add butter and milk to the mash, continuing to mash until smooth.
   Season with salt and black pepper to taste.

3. Assemble Tacos:

Warm tortillas according to package instructions.
Spread a layer of neeps and tatties mash onto each tortilla.
Spoon the haggis filling over the mash.
Garnish with chopped fresh chives or parsley.
Optionally, drizzle with whisky sauce or your favorite hot sauce for extra flavor.

4. Serve:

Enjoy your Scottish Haggis Tacos with Neeps and Tatties Mash immediately. The combination of the rich and savory haggis, the creamy neeps and tatties mash, and the optional whisky sauce create a unique and delicious taco experience with Scottish flair.

Peruvian Ceviche Tacos with Aji Amarillo Crema

Ingredients:

For the Ceviche:

- 1 pound white fish fillets, diced into small pieces
- 1 cup fresh lime juice
- 1 red onion, thinly sliced
- 1-2 jalapeños, seeded and finely chopped
- 1 cup cherry tomatoes, halved
- 1/2 cup fresh cilantro, chopped
- Salt and black pepper to taste

For the Aji Amarillo Crema:

- 1/2 cup mayonnaise
- 1-2 tablespoons Aji Amarillo paste (adjust to taste)
- 1 tablespoon fresh lime juice
- Salt to taste

For Tacos:

- Small flour or corn tortillas
- Shredded iceberg lettuce or cabbage
- Sliced avocado
- Fresh cilantro leaves for garnish
- Lime wedges for serving

Instructions:

1. Prepare Ceviche:

   In a bowl, combine diced white fish, fresh lime juice, thinly sliced red onion, chopped jalapeños, cherry tomatoes, chopped cilantro, salt, and black pepper.
   Mix well to ensure the fish is coated in lime juice. Cover and refrigerate for at least 30 minutes or until the fish turns opaque.

2. Prepare Aji Amarillo Crema:

   In a small bowl, whisk together mayonnaise, Aji Amarillo paste, fresh lime juice, and salt. Adjust the amount of Aji Amarillo paste according to your desired level of spiciness.

3. Assemble Tacos:

   Warm tortillas according to package instructions.
   Place shredded iceberg lettuce or cabbage onto each tortilla.
   Spoon the ceviche mixture over the lettuce.
   Drizzle Aji Amarillo crema over the ceviche.

Top with sliced avocado.
Garnish with fresh cilantro leaves.
Serve with lime wedges on the side.

4. Serve:

Enjoy your Peruvian Ceviche Tacos with Aji Amarillo Crema immediately. The combination of the zesty ceviche, creamy Aji Amarillo crema, and fresh toppings create a delightful and flavorful taco experience with Peruvian influences.

German Sauerbraten Tacos with Red Cabbage Slaw

Ingredients:

For the Sauerbraten Filling:

- 1 1/2 pounds beef roast (such as chuck or rump)
- 1 large onion, sliced
- 2 cloves garlic, minced
- 1 cup red wine vinegar
- 1 cup beef broth
- 1/2 cup red wine
- 1/4 cup brown sugar
- 10 whole peppercorns
- 4 cloves
- 2 bay leaves
- Salt and black pepper to taste
- 2 tablespoons vegetable oil for searing

For the Red Cabbage Slaw:

- 2 cups shredded red cabbage
- 1 apple, julienned
- 1/4 cup apple cider vinegar
- 1 tablespoon honey
- 1 tablespoon Dijon mustard
- 2 tablespoons olive oil
- Salt and black pepper to taste

For Tacos:

- Small flour or corn tortillas
- Dill pickles or gherkins, sliced
- Fresh parsley, chopped (for garnish)

Instructions:

1. Prepare Sauerbraten Filling:

>In a large bowl, combine sliced onion, minced garlic, red wine vinegar, beef broth, red wine, brown sugar, peppercorns, cloves, bay leaves, salt, and black pepper. Place the beef roast in the marinade, ensuring it's fully submerged. Cover and refrigerate for at least 24-48 hours, turning the meat occasionally.
>Preheat the oven to 325°F (163°C).
>Remove the beef from the marinade and pat it dry with paper towels.
>In an ovenproof pot, heat vegetable oil over medium-high heat. Sear the beef on all sides until browned.

Pour the marinade over the beef, cover the pot, and transfer it to the preheated oven.
Cook for 2-3 hours or until the beef is tender and can be easily shredded.

2. Prepare Red Cabbage Slaw:

In a bowl, combine shredded red cabbage and julienned apple.
In a small bowl, whisk together apple cider vinegar, honey, Dijon mustard, olive oil, salt, and black pepper.
Pour the dressing over the cabbage and apple mixture. Toss to combine.
Refrigerate until ready to use.

3. Assemble Tacos:

Warm tortillas according to package instructions.
Shred the sauerbraten beef and place it onto each tortilla.
Top with red cabbage slaw.
Add sliced dill pickles or gherkins.
Garnish with chopped fresh parsley.

4. Serve:

Enjoy your German Sauerbraten Tacos with Red Cabbage Slaw immediately. The combination of tender sauerbraten, crunchy red cabbage slaw, and tangy pickles create a unique and flavorful taco experience with German influences.

Nigerian Jollof Rice Tacos with Spicy Tomato Relish

Ingredients:

For the Jollof Rice:

- 2 cups long-grain parboiled rice
- 1/4 cup vegetable oil
- 1 onion, finely chopped
- 2 red bell peppers, blended
- 3 tomatoes, blended
- 2 cloves garlic, minced
- 1 teaspoon thyme
- 1 teaspoon curry powder
- 1 teaspoon paprika
- 1 bay leaf
- Salt and black pepper to taste
- 2 cups chicken or vegetable broth

For the Spicy Tomato Relish:

- 1 cup cherry tomatoes, halved
- 1 red onion, finely chopped
- 1 jalapeño, seeds removed and finely chopped
- 2 tablespoons fresh cilantro, chopped
- 1 tablespoon lime juice
- Salt to taste

For Tacos:

- Small flour or corn tortillas
- Shredded lettuce or cabbage
- Avocado slices
- Fresh cilantro leaves for garnish
- Lime wedges for serving

Instructions:

1. Prepare Jollof Rice:

   Rinse the rice under cold water until the water runs clear. Drain and set aside.
   In a large skillet or pot, heat vegetable oil over medium heat.
   Add chopped onions and sauté until softened.
   Add minced garlic, blended red bell peppers, blended tomatoes, thyme, curry powder, paprika, bay leaf, salt, and black pepper. Cook for about 10 minutes, stirring occasionally.
   Add the drained rice to the skillet and stir to coat the rice with the tomato mixture.
   Pour in chicken or vegetable broth, bring to a boil, then reduce heat to low. Cover and simmer until the rice is cooked and the liquid is absorbed.

2. Prepare Spicy Tomato Relish:

> In a bowl, combine halved cherry tomatoes, chopped red onion, chopped jalapeño, chopped fresh cilantro, lime juice, and salt. Mix well.

3. Assemble Tacos:

> Warm tortillas according to package instructions.
> Place shredded lettuce or cabbage onto each tortilla.
> Spoon Jollof rice onto the lettuce.
> Top with spicy tomato relish.
> Add avocado slices.
> Garnish with fresh cilantro leaves.
> Serve with lime wedges on the side.

4. Serve:

Enjoy your Nigerian Jollof Rice Tacos with Spicy Tomato Relish immediately. The combination of flavorful Jollof rice and the zesty tomato relish creates a unique and delicious taco experience with Nigerian influences.

Swiss Fondue Tacos with Gruyère and Caramelized Onions

Ingredients:

For the Fondue:

- 2 cups Gruyère cheese, grated
- 1 cup Emmental cheese, grated
- 1 clove garlic, halved
- 1 cup dry white wine
- 1 tablespoon lemon juice
- 1 tablespoon cornstarch
- 1 tablespoon kirsch (cherry brandy)
- Nutmeg, freshly grated (to taste)
- Salt and white pepper to taste

For Caramelized Onions:

- 2 large onions, thinly sliced
- 2 tablespoons butter
- 1 tablespoon olive oil
- Salt and black pepper to taste

For Tacos:

- Small flour or corn tortillas
- Fresh parsley, chopped (for garnish)
- Cornichons or pickles, sliced (for serving)

Instructions:

1. Prepare Fondue:

   Rub the inside of a fondue pot with the halved garlic clove.
   In a bowl, toss the grated Gruyère and Emmental with cornstarch until well coated.
   In the fondue pot, heat white wine over medium heat until hot but not boiling.
   Gradually add the cheese mixture, stirring continuously in a figure-eight motion until the cheese is melted and smooth.
   Stir in lemon juice, kirsch, and freshly grated nutmeg.
   Season with salt and white pepper to taste.
   Keep the fondue warm over a low flame.

2. Prepare Caramelized Onions:

   In a skillet, heat butter and olive oil over medium-low heat.
   Add thinly sliced onions and cook slowly until caramelized, stirring occasionally.

Season with salt and black pepper to taste.

3. Assemble Tacos:

    Warm tortillas according to package instructions.
    Spoon a generous amount of Swiss fondue onto each tortilla.
    Top with a spoonful of caramelized onions.
    Garnish with chopped fresh parsley.

4. Serve:

Enjoy your Swiss Fondue Tacos with Gruyère and Caramelized Onions immediately. The combination of rich, melty fondue and sweet caramelized onions creates a decadent and delightful taco experience with Swiss flair. Serve with sliced cornichons or pickles on the side for added freshness.

Thai Massaman Curry Beef Tacos with Peanut Crunch

Ingredients:

For the Massaman Curry Beef:

- 1 pound beef sirloin, thinly sliced
- 2 tablespoons Massaman curry paste
- 1 can (13.5 oz) coconut milk
- 1 onion, sliced
- 2 potatoes, peeled and diced
- 1 cup beef or vegetable broth
- 2 tablespoons fish sauce
- 1 tablespoon tamarind paste
- 1 tablespoon brown sugar
- Salt to taste
- Chopped fresh cilantro for garnish

For the Peanut Crunch:

- 1/2 cup roasted peanuts, chopped
- 1 tablespoon sesame seeds
- 1 tablespoon honey
- Pinch of salt

For Tacos:

- Small flour or corn tortillas
- Shredded lettuce or cabbage
- Sliced cucumber
- Lime wedges for serving

Instructions:

1. Prepare Massaman Curry Beef:

   In a large skillet or pot, heat a bit of oil over medium heat. Add Massaman curry paste and sauté for a minute until fragrant.
   Add sliced beef and cook until browned on all sides.
   Pour in coconut milk, beef or vegetable broth, fish sauce, tamarind paste, and brown sugar. Stir to combine.
   Add sliced onions and diced potatoes to the skillet. Simmer until the potatoes are tender and the beef is cooked through.
   Season with salt to taste. Remove from heat and set aside.

2. Prepare Peanut Crunch:

   In a small bowl, mix chopped roasted peanuts, sesame seeds, honey, and a pinch of salt. Set aside.

3. Assemble Tacos:

> Warm tortillas according to package instructions.
> Place shredded lettuce or cabbage onto each tortilla.
> Spoon Massaman curry beef onto the lettuce.
> Top with sliced cucumber.
> Sprinkle Peanut Crunch over the beef.
> Garnish with chopped fresh cilantro.
> Serve with lime wedges on the side.

4. Serve:

Enjoy your Thai Massaman Curry Beef Tacos with Peanut Crunch immediately. The combination of rich Massaman curry beef, crunchy peanuts, and fresh veggies creates a delicious and exotic taco experience with Thai flair.

Turkish Lahmacun-Inspired Lamb Tacos with Sumac Yogurt

Ingredients:

For the Spiced Lamb:

- 1 pound ground lamb
- 1 onion, finely chopped
- 2 cloves garlic, minced

- 2 tomatoes, diced
- 1/4 cup tomato paste
- 1 tablespoon ground cumin
- 1 tablespoon ground coriander
- 1 teaspoon paprika
- 1/2 teaspoon cayenne pepper (adjust to taste)
- Salt and black pepper to taste
- Olive oil for cooking

For the Sumac Yogurt:

- 1 cup Greek yogurt
- 1 tablespoon olive oil
- 1 teaspoon sumac
- Salt to taste

For Tacos:

- Small flour or corn tortillas
- Finely chopped fresh parsley or cilantro for garnish
- Sliced radishes for garnish
- Lemon wedges for serving

Instructions:

1. Prepare Spiced Lamb:

   In a skillet, heat olive oil over medium heat. Add chopped onions and cook until softened.
   Add minced garlic and ground lamb to the skillet. Cook until the lamb is browned.
   Stir in diced tomatoes, tomato paste, ground cumin, ground coriander, paprika, cayenne pepper, salt, and black pepper. Cook until the tomatoes are softened and the mixture is well combined.
   Remove from heat and set aside.

2. Prepare Sumac Yogurt:

   In a bowl, mix Greek yogurt, olive oil, sumac, and salt. Adjust the seasoning to taste.

3. Assemble Tacos:

   Warm tortillas according to package instructions.
   Spoon spiced lamb mixture onto each tortilla.

Drizzle sumac yogurt over the lamb.
Garnish with finely chopped fresh parsley or cilantro.
Add sliced radishes for extra crunch.
Serve with lemon wedges on the side.

4. Serve:

Enjoy your Turkish Lahmacun-Inspired Lamb Tacos with Sumac Yogurt immediately. The combination of flavorful spiced lamb, tangy sumac yogurt, and fresh garnishes create a delicious and unique taco experience with Turkish influences.

Polish Pierogi Tacos with Potato and Cheddar Filling

Ingredients:

For the Potato and Cheddar Filling:

- 2 cups mashed potatoes
- 1 cup shredded cheddar cheese
- 1 onion, finely chopped and sautéed until caramelized

- Salt and black pepper to taste

For the Tacos:

- Small flour or corn tortillas
- Sour cream for drizzling
- Chopped chives or green onions for garnish
- Cooked and crumbled bacon (optional)
- Sauerkraut for topping (optional)

Instructions:

1. Prepare Potato and Cheddar Filling:

    In a bowl, mix mashed potatoes, shredded cheddar cheese, and sautéed caramelized onions.
    Season with salt and black pepper to taste. Set aside.

2. Assemble Tacos:

    Warm tortillas according to package instructions.
    Spoon the potato and cheddar filling onto each tortilla.
    Drizzle with sour cream.
    Garnish with chopped chives or green onions.
    Optionally, top with cooked and crumbled bacon for added flavor.
    For a traditional touch, you can also add a spoonful of sauerkraut on top.

3. Serve:

Enjoy your Polish Pierogi Tacos with Potato and Cheddar Filling immediately. The combination of creamy potato and cheddar filling with the taco format creates a unique and delicious taco experience with Polish influences.

Brazilian Moqueca Tacos with Coconut-Lime Drizzle

Ingredients:

For the Moqueca Filling:

- 1 pound white fish fillets (such as cod or snapper), cut into bite-sized pieces
- 1 pound shrimp, peeled and deveined

- 1 onion, thinly sliced
- 1 bell pepper, thinly sliced
- 2 tomatoes, diced
- 3 cloves garlic, minced
- 1 tablespoon olive oil
- 1 can (14 oz) coconut milk
- 1 cup fish or vegetable broth
- 2 tablespoons tomato paste
- 1 tablespoon palm oil (dende oil) for authenticity (optional)
- 1 tablespoon lime juice
- 1 teaspoon paprika
- 1 teaspoon cayenne pepper (adjust to taste)
- Salt and black pepper to taste
- Fresh cilantro, chopped (for garnish)

For the Coconut-Lime Drizzle:

- 1/2 cup coconut cream
- 2 tablespoons lime juice
- Zest of one lime
- Salt to taste

For Tacos:

- Small flour or corn tortillas
- Shredded cabbage or lettuce
- Sliced avocado
- Lime wedges for serving

Instructions:

1. Prepare Moqueca Filling:

In a large skillet or pot, heat olive oil over medium heat. Add sliced onions and bell peppers, sauté until softened.
Add minced garlic and cook for another minute.
Stir in diced tomatoes, coconut milk, fish or vegetable broth, tomato paste, palm oil (if using), lime juice, paprika, cayenne pepper, salt, and black pepper. Bring to a simmer.
Add fish and shrimp to the simmering broth. Cook until the seafood is cooked through and flavors are well combined.
Adjust seasoning to taste. Remove from heat and set aside.

2. Prepare Coconut-Lime Drizzle:

   In a bowl, whisk together coconut cream, lime juice, lime zest, and salt. Set aside.

3. Assemble Tacos:

   Warm tortillas according to package instructions.
   Place shredded cabbage or lettuce onto each tortilla.
   Spoon the moqueca filling (fish and shrimp) onto the cabbage.
   Top with sliced avocado.
   Drizzle with coconut-lime drizzle.
   Garnish with fresh chopped cilantro.
   Serve with lime wedges on the side.

4. Serve:

Enjoy your Brazilian Moqueca Tacos with Coconut-Lime Drizzle immediately. The combination of the rich and coconut-infused moqueca, the zesty coconut-lime drizzle, and fresh toppings create a delicious and exotic taco experience with Brazilian flair.

Hawaiian Loco Moco Tacos with Sunny-Side-Up Egg

Ingredients:

For the Hamburger Patties:

- 1 pound ground beef
- Salt and black pepper to taste
- 1 tablespoon Worcestershire sauce

- 1 teaspoon garlic powder
- 1 teaspoon onion powder

For the Brown Gravy:

- 2 tablespoons butter
- 2 tablespoons all-purpose flour
- 2 cups beef or chicken broth
- 1 tablespoon soy sauce
- Salt and black pepper to taste

For the Tacos:

- Small flour or corn tortillas
- Cooked white rice
- Sunny-side-up eggs (1 per taco)
- Chopped green onions for garnish

Instructions:

1. Prepare Hamburger Patties:

   In a bowl, mix ground beef with salt, black pepper, Worcestershire sauce, garlic powder, and onion powder.
   Form the mixture into small hamburger patties.
   Cook the patties in a skillet or on a grill until they reach your desired level of doneness.

2. Prepare Brown Gravy:

   In a saucepan, melt butter over medium heat.
   Add all-purpose flour and whisk continuously to create a roux.
   Gradually pour in beef or chicken broth, continuing to whisk to avoid lumps.
   Stir in soy sauce, salt, and black pepper.
   Cook the gravy until it thickens to your desired consistency.

3. Assemble Tacos:

   Warm tortillas according to package instructions.
   Place a spoonful of cooked white rice onto each tortilla.
   Put a hamburger patty on top of the rice.
   Spoon brown gravy generously over the hamburger patty.
   Fry sunny-side-up eggs and place one on each taco.
   Garnish with chopped green onions.

4. Serve:

Enjoy your Hawaiian Loco Moco Tacos with Sunny-Side-Up Egg immediately. The combination of the savory hamburger patty, rice, rich brown gravy, and a runny egg yolk creates a unique and delicious taco experience with Hawaiian-inspired flavors.

Moroccan Lamb Tagine Tacos with Apricot Chutney

Ingredients:

For the Lamb Tagine:
- 1 1/2 pounds lamb shoulder, cut into cubes
- 2 tablespoons olive oil

- 1 onion, finely chopped
- 3 cloves garlic, minced
- 1 teaspoon ground cumin
- 1 teaspoon ground coriander
- 1 teaspoon ground cinnamon
- 1 teaspoon paprika
- 1/2 teaspoon ground ginger
- 1/2 teaspoon ground turmeric
- Salt and black pepper to taste
- 1 can (14 oz) diced tomatoes
- 1/2 cup dried apricots, chopped
- 1/4 cup slivered almonds, toasted
- Fresh cilantro, chopped (for garnish)

For the Apricot Chutney:

- 1 cup dried apricots, chopped
- 1/2 cup red onion, finely chopped
- 1/4 cup apple cider vinegar
- 2 tablespoons honey
- 1 teaspoon ground cumin
- 1/2 teaspoon red pepper flakes (adjust to taste)
- Salt to taste

For Tacos:

- Small flour or corn tortillas
- Shredded lettuce or cabbage
- Sliced cucumber
- Greek yogurt or tzatziki for drizzling

Instructions:

1. Prepare Lamb Tagine:

> In a Dutch oven or large skillet, heat olive oil over medium heat. Add chopped onions and cook until softened.
> Add minced garlic and cook for an additional minute.
> Add cubed lamb shoulder to the skillet and brown on all sides.
> Stir in ground cumin, ground coriander, ground cinnamon, paprika, ground ginger, ground turmeric, salt, and black pepper. Cook for 2-3 minutes until the spices are fragrant.
> Pour in diced tomatoes and chopped dried apricots. Stir to combine.

Cover and simmer for about 1.5 to 2 hours or until the lamb is tender.
In the last 15 minutes of cooking, add toasted slivered almonds. Adjust seasoning if necessary.

2. Prepare Apricot Chutney:

In a saucepan, combine chopped dried apricots, finely chopped red onion, apple cider vinegar, honey, ground cumin, red pepper flakes, and salt.
Simmer over medium heat until the chutney thickens and the apricots are softened.
Adjust sweetness and spice levels to your liking.

3. Assemble Tacos:

Warm tortillas according to package instructions.
Place shredded lettuce or cabbage onto each tortilla.
Spoon the Moroccan lamb tagine onto the lettuce.
Top with sliced cucumber.
Drizzle with Greek yogurt or tzatziki.
Spoon apricot chutney generously over the lamb.
Garnish with chopped fresh cilantro.

4. Serve:

Enjoy your Moroccan Lamb Tagine Tacos with Apricot Chutney immediately. The combination of spiced lamb, sweet apricot chutney, and fresh toppings create a unique and delicious taco experience with Moroccan influences.

Filipino Halo-Halo Tacos with Ube Ice Cream

Ingredients:

For the Halo-Halo Filling:

- Shaved ice
- Sweetened condensed milk
- Evaporated milk
- Leche flan (Filipino caramel custard)
- Ube halaya (purple yam jam)
- Sweetened red beans
- Sweetened coconut strips
- Nata de coco (coconut jelly)
- Jackfruit, thinly sliced
- Cornflakes or rice crispies

For the Ube Ice Cream:

- 2 cups heavy cream
- 1 cup whole milk
- 3/4 cup granulated sugar
- 1/2 cup ube halaya (purple yam jam)
- 1 teaspoon vanilla extract
- A pinch of salt

For Tacos:

- Small flour or corn tortillas

Instructions:

1. Prepare Ube Ice Cream:

   In a medium saucepan, combine heavy cream, whole milk, and granulated sugar. Heat over medium heat until the mixture is warm and the sugar is dissolved.
   Whisk in ube halaya (purple yam jam) until fully incorporated.
   Remove from heat and stir in vanilla extract and a pinch of salt.
   Allow the mixture to cool completely, then refrigerate for at least 4 hours or overnight.
   Churn the mixture in an ice cream maker according to the manufacturer's instructions.
   Transfer the churned ice cream to a lidded container and freeze until firm.

2. Assemble Tacos:

   Warm tortillas according to package instructions.
   Assemble the tacos by filling each tortilla with shaved ice.
   Drizzle sweetened condensed milk and evaporated milk over the ice.

Add leche flan, ube halaya, sweetened red beans, sweetened coconut strips, nata de coco, thinly sliced jackfruit, and cornflakes or rice crispies on top of the ice.
Top each taco with a scoop of homemade ube ice cream.

3. Serve:

Enjoy your Filipino Halo-Halo Tacos with Ube Ice Cream immediately. The combination of halo-halo ingredients in a taco with the creamy and vibrant ube ice cream creates a unique and delightful dessert experience with Filipino flair.

Canadian Butter Tart Tacos with Pecans and Maple Syrup

Ingredients:

For the Butter Tart Filling:

- 1/2 cup unsalted butter, melted
- 1 cup packed brown sugar
- 2 large eggs
- 1 teaspoon vanilla extract
- 1/4 cup all-purpose flour
- 1/4 teaspoon baking powder
- 1/4 teaspoon salt
- 1/2 cup chopped pecans

For the Tacos:

- Small flour or corn tortillas
- Pecan halves (for garnish)
- Maple syrup for drizzling
- Whipped cream or vanilla ice cream (optional)

Instructions:

1. Prepare Butter Tart Filling:

    Preheat your oven to 350°F (175°C).
    In a bowl, whisk together melted butter, brown sugar, eggs, and vanilla extract until well combined.
    Add all-purpose flour, baking powder, and salt to the mixture. Stir until smooth.
    Fold in the chopped pecans.

2. Assemble Tacos:

    Warm tortillas according to package instructions.
    Shape each tortilla into a taco shell or use pre-made taco shells.
    Spoon the butter tart filling into each taco shell.
    Place pecan halves on top of the filling for garnish.
    Bake in the preheated oven for about 12-15 minutes or until the filling is set and the edges are golden brown.

3. Drizzle and Serve:

    Remove the butter tart tacos from the oven.
    Drizzle each taco with maple syrup.
    Optionally, top with whipped cream or a scoop of vanilla ice cream for an extra indulgence.

Serve the Canadian Butter Tart Tacos with Pecans and Maple Syrup warm.

4. Enjoy:

Enjoy your Canadian Butter Tart Tacos with Pecans and Maple Syrup as a delightful Canadian-inspired dessert. The combination of the gooey butter tart filling, crunchy pecans, and sweet maple syrup in a taco form creates a delicious and indulgent treat.

Malaysian Nasi Lemak Tacos with Sambal Belacan

Ingredients:

For Nasi Lemak Filling:

- 2 cups cooked coconut rice (Nasi Lemak style, with pandan leaves if available)
- 1 cup fried anchovies (ikan bilis)
- 1 cup roasted peanuts
- 4 hard-boiled eggs, sliced
- Fresh cucumber, julienned

For Sambal Belacan:

- 10-12 red chilies, seeded and chopped
- 4 shallots, chopped
- 3 cloves garlic, chopped
- 1 tablespoon belacan (shrimp paste), roasted
- 2 tablespoons tamarind paste
- 2 tablespoons sugar
- Salt to taste
- Cooking oil

For Tacos:

- Small taco-sized flour tortillas or corn tortillas

Optional Garnishes:

- Fresh cilantro, chopped
- Lime wedges

Instructions:

1. Prepare Nasi Lemak Filling:

a. Cook coconut rice using pandan leaves for added aroma.

b. In a pan, fry anchovies until crispy. Drain excess oil on paper towels.

c. Roast peanuts until golden brown.

2. Make Sambal Belacan:

a. Blend red chilies, shallots, garlic, and roasted belacan into a smooth paste.

b. Heat oil in a pan, sauté the paste until fragrant.

c. Add tamarind paste, sugar, and salt. Cook until the sambal thickens.

3. Assemble Tacos:

a. Warm tortillas in a dry pan or microwave.

b. Place a spoonful of coconut rice in the center of each tortilla.

c. Top with fried anchovies, roasted peanuts, sliced hard-boiled eggs, and julienned cucumber.

4. Drizzle with Sambal Belacan:

a. Generously spoon sambal belacan over the Nasi Lemak filling.

5. Garnish and Serve:

a. Garnish with fresh cilantro and serve with lime wedges on the side.

b. Optionally, add more sambal for extra heat.

Enjoy your Malaysian Nasi Lemak Tacos with Sambal Belacan!

Feel free to adjust the spice levels and ingredients according to your taste preferences. This fusion dish brings together the comforting flavors of Nasi Lemak with the fun and convenient taco form, making it a perfect blend of Malaysian and international cuisine.